WALKS AROUND TELFORD

Fourteen Country Walks from Telford's Doorstep

David Gregory

EXPLORING SHROPSHIRE

with
Shropshire Books

EXPLORING SHROPSHIRE

WALKS AROUND TELFORD forms part of a series of books and leaflets on walking published by Shropshire Books known as Exploring Shropshire. For other titles in the series see page 82.

Front cover: Blue Pool, Telford Town Park. Photograph by Gordon Dickins

ISBN: 0-903802-65-1

© David Gregory 1995, revised reprint 2003

Cover and Book design: Daywell Designs

Illustrations: Kathryn Green

Managing Editor: Helen Sample

Published by Shropshire Books, the publishing Division of the Information and Community Services Department of Shropshire County Council.

Printed in Great Britain by Livesey Ltd.

CONTENTS

INTRODUCTION

The name Telford New Town may well conjure up an image of impersonal, modern housing and massive industrial estates blanketing the landscape. However, neither the Industrial Revolution of the eighteenth and nineteenth centuries nor the more recent development of the new town have been able to rob the area of its rich heritage of attractive and varied countryside. The rolling acres of Telford Town Park allow the natural world to flourish within the heart of the town itself, whilst a short road journey from the Town Centre quickly leads to quiet country lanes, lonely field pathways, secluded woodland and meandering streams frequently backed by pleasing views of distant hills.

I hope this book will help visitors and residents alike to find and enjoy some of the best features of the rural landscape both within and around Telford. If the reader also finds peace and refreshment together with a deeper appreciation of the area's character and history, the aims of this work will have been fully achieved.

On a cautionary note - pathways can quickly become muddy after rain, undergrowth can become rampant in high summer, and there will be fences and gates to climb. Nevertheless, armed with the right clothing and footwear, the walker should not have difficulty carrying out the walks. Despite the inclusion of several villages around the Telford area, the walks do not often encompass a village shop or 'water-hole', so it may be advisable to carry a snack to sustain you along your way.

I have gratefully received a good deal of help and guidance from various people on my way around the walks. In addition, I owe a debt of thanks to all those who have supplied me with essential background information relating to some of the locations. In particular, I would like to thank local historian Mr Ken Jones, of Little Wenlock, Mr and Mrs Neil Dobson, Wall Farm, Kynnersley, Mr Henry White, Cold Hatton, Mrs M Afia, Hatton Grange, Shifnal, Nigel Jones of the County Council Countryside Service for supplying me with maps, Helen Sample, Managing Editor, Shropshire Books for her help and encouragement and to my wife, May, for all the help and support she has given.

Dave Gregory   January 1995

KEY TO MAPS

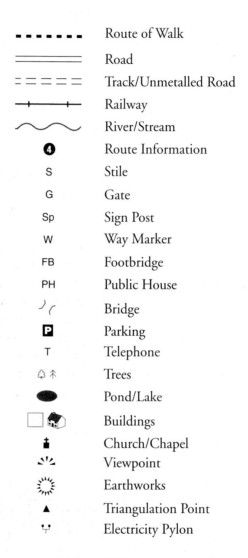

- - - - - -	Route of Walk
══════	Road
= = = =	Track/Unmetalled Road
—┼——┼—	Railway
∿	River/Stream
❹	Route Information
S	Stile
G	Gate
Sp	Sign Post
W	Way Marker
FB	Footbridge
PH	Public House
⌐⌐	Bridge
P	Parking
T	Telephone
♧ 禾	Trees
⬤	Pond/Lake
▢ 🏠	Buildings
♗	Church/Chapel
﹀	Viewpoint
☼	Earthworks
▲	Triangulation Point
Ψ	Electricity Pylon

Rights of Way

Every care has been taken to ensure the accuracy of the maps and route descriptions. If a right of way is obstructed the facts should be reported to the Countryside Section of Shropshire County Council.

Kynnersley - Wall Farm - Kynnersley

O.S. Map 1:50,000 Sheet No. 127 Starting Point: GR 673 167
Parking: roadside near Kynnersley Church. Distance: 3 miles.

A fairly easy walk through relatively flat countryside, chiefly using broad trackways and field paths and including a visit to an impressive, lowland Iron-age fort.

Kynnersley lies at the very heart of the Weald (or 'wild') moors, a great expanse of former marshland drained during the nineteenth century by no less a personage than Thomas Telford for the benefit of the main landowner of the area, the first Duke of Sutherland. The former marshes were a legacy of the ice ages and although ancient woodland once covered the landscape, the region was of little use for cultivation until the worthy duke had it drained. The present-day landscape is mainly flat yet full of character and interest. Something of the aura of the Sutherland epoch lives on in the distinctive cottages, impressive farmhouses and remote, open countryside which still characterise the area.

The village of Kynnersley suffered a catastrophic fire in 1791 and although little remains of the old village, it nevertheless retains an air of tranquil remoteness, as if happy to be distanced from the rest of the world. There are some attractive cottages and one or two elegant old houses. There is a raised, triangular piece of ground near the church called The Whym (a Whym was a horse or steam-powered windlass used in mining). It has also been suggested that the orchard of the nearby Whym Cottage is the site of an old

St. Chad's Church

1

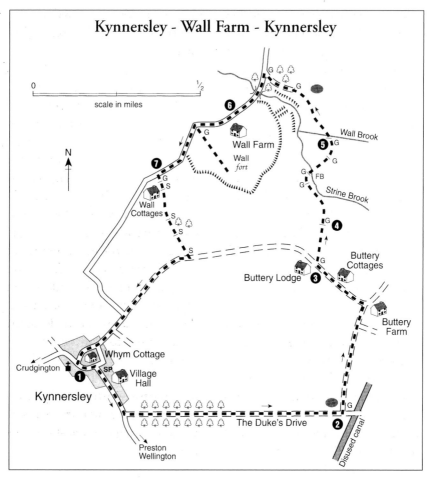

Kynnersley - Wall Farm - Kynnersley

0 ½
scale in miles

N

Wall Brook

6

Wall Farm

Wall *fort*

5 G

7

G
S

Wall
Cottages

S

S

G
G FB
G
Strine Brook

S

G
4

Buttery
Cottages

G

Buttery Lodge **3**

Buttery
Farm

Whym Cottage

Crudgington

SP

Village
Hall

Kynnersley

The Duke's Drive

2

G

Disused canal

Preston
Wellington

1

---

burial ground for criminals executed for such misdemeanours as sheep-stealing in bygone days. The small, Early English church of St. Chad at the centre of the village is of considerable interest. The main body of the building is of stone and originally had a thatched roof. It was built in the thirteenth century on the site of an earlier chapel. The tower, added in 1694,

includes some Norman stones. An odd feature is the double bell-cot located at the junction of chancel and the nave.

1. From the church walk along pavement past Kynnersley House Farm and towards signpost at road junction. Turn right. Follow sign 'Preston, Wellington' and pass Village Hall on left. At the end of

village, turn left on to unmetalled roadway. The roadway runs in a generally straight direction between trees. Eventually, a shallow stream can be seen down a dip to the right with woodland beyond.

The roadway is still known locally as 'The Duke's Drive' and was built with an almost Roman straightness by Sutherland during the last century. It runs for about six miles from his residence at Lilleshall Hall to the western extremity of his estate near Crudgington.

2. Shortly before the drive reaches a section of the disused Newport branch of the Shropshire Union Canal, turn left through a metal gate and on to a trackway which soon passes an attractive pool with a reedbed and tree-covered island on the left. The trackway takes you between fields and soon Buttery Farm can be seen ahead on the right. As you approach the imposing farmhouse another trackway from Buttery Bridge joins you on the right-hand side. Keep straight ahead until reaching a T-junction at which you turn left on to a farm lane cutting between open fields. Ahead, lies a remote cluster of Duke of Sutherland cottages. After passing Buttery

Cottages on the right, look out for Buttery Lodge further on and to the left.

Many local placenames ending in the suffix 'y' or 'ey' as in Buttery or Kynnersley are based on a Saxon word for 'island', denoting that these ancient settlements were once raised oases of land surrounded by the former wetland terrain. No longer wild and wet, this area of fertile fields and scattered cottages and farms nevertheless retains an air of timelessness and the distinctive cottages of red brick, with gabled upper windows and short, dark-tiled roofs, almost cause the spirit of the Duke to preside over the area, still.

3. Opposite Buttery Lodge turn right through a wooden gateway and walk along the right-hand side of a field.

You are now walking (with free consent) on land belonging to the owners of Wall Farm. The fields through which you will be walking became subject in 1994, to a government supported stewardship scheme encouraging agricultural landowners to hive-off a proportion of their acreage for the growing of threatened species of grasses and, in fact, establish an environment

3

somewhat akin to that of one hundred years ago. All credit is due to Mr Neil Dobson, the farmer in question, for his enlightened attitude to conservation which also includes the planting of numerous varieties of native trees, preserving an historic site situated on his land, and, of course, granting the rambler easy access to his part of the countryside.

4. Go through another wooden gate and into the next field, keeping the fence on your right. Follow the field edge as it turns to the left and goes along the left-hand side of the Strine Brook. At the field edge, there is a slight rise in the ground - this is part of a pre-historic fort which is visited more fully a little later in the walk. Look for a wooden gate to the right and thereby enter next field. In a few yards, turn right through a wooden gate and cross the Strine, using a wooden footbridge. You have now entered a further outpost of the ancient monument. Bear right, following the fence and make for the wooden gate, ignoring wide metal gate. Undulations in the field to the right are part of the fort. Go through the gate into the next field and walk along the right hand side. At the field edge, follow the fence round to the left.

The soil hereabouts is very dark and peaty and if the farmer's policy is working, there should be some evidence of the natural regeneration of various grasses which it is hoped will also encourage the return of certain wading birds. Within these fields have been found stones which it is thought were used by ancient man in the process of heating water. Because the earthenware pots then used were incapable of resisting high temperatures, the small stones were first heated on a fire, then placed inside a jug of water to produce hot water.

5. At the field edge, go through the gate, cross a footbridge and further gate into the next field, walking along the right-hand side. Beyond this field can be seen an old, stone cattle shelter. Follow the field edge as it turns left.

Wall Brook runs alongside the field on the right-hand and is a favourite haunt of heron. A gap in the trees to the right affords a view of Tibberton Grange standing impressively at the top of the slope.

After an attractive pool on the right go through a wide gate and on to a broad track between fields. Stay on this track as it passes a small copse on the right. Where the track curves to the right, go

through the gate and turn left on to a metalled lane. Walk along the lane between trees and then a stone bridge crosses the River Strine. From this point, the lane passes for a short distance over more of the outer ramparts of the fort and there are further undulations in the field to the right. Wall Farm and its attractive farmhouse come into view on the left-hand side of the road.

Wall Farm stands next to a low sandstone bank on and around which is situated one of the largest surviving lowland, iron age camps in the country. The main body of the fort comprises a natural island of some 61 hectares and is enclosed by a series of banks and ditches, some of them encountered in the fields earlier in the walk. It is thought likely that the site was used as a transit camp for the movement of livestock from the mountainous Western regions on a seasonal basis, and it might, perhaps, even predate the iron-age. There is evidence of extensive occupation in the pre-Roman period and of the camp's defensive function. A selection of the artefacts recovered on or near the site over the years includes a flint arrowhead, a Celtic bead (found in the peat), large rocks conveyed from other parts, evidence of the water-heating process using pebbles and charcoal fires, the postholes of wooden huts, fragments of pre-historic pottery, Roman coins and a fourteenth century basalt hone.

6. Continue along the lane for a short distance and as the road bears right go through the wide, wooden gate on the left (bearing a sign with a white arrow on a green circle). Walk for about 100 yards alongside the fence to get a good look at the impressive earthworks of grass-covered banks guarding the large, central section of the fort (N.B. be sure to stay alongside the fence as walking on the actual site is not allowed). Retrace your steps to the lane and turn left along the road where you will soon reach

Whym Cottage

more Duke of Sutherland cottages known as Wall Cottages on the left.

7. Turn left immediately before reaching the cottages and climb a stile, walking to the left of Wall Brook. At the field end, climb a stile and walk to the right of a group of trees. Climb a further stile and walk along a field path still to the left of the stream. Climb another stile and turn right on to an unmetalled lane. At the top of the hill, the buildings of Kynnersley come into view ahead. The lane soon joins a metalled road. Go straight ahead and into Kynnersley. Distant views of Lilleshall Hill and the Wrekin can be seen as you approach the Kynnersley sign. At a junction at which Briar Patch Cottage stands to the left, and New Villas are to the right, cross over to a side road ignoring the main thoroughfare which bears left. At a black and white, half-timbered cottage (Whym Cottage) take the left fork to St. Chad's Church.

All Round the Wrekin

O.S. Map 1:50,000 Sheet No 127
Starting Point: GR 637 094. Roadside near reservoir at foot of Wrekin.
Parking on verge of road which comes from M54 - Junction 7,
via Cluddley to the Wrekin. Distance: 3 miles

A walk along well-made paths around the base of the Wrekin. There is a fairly steep and sometimes rocky climb at the beginning of the walk but the paths generally undulate more gently. There is a mixture of woodland and intermittent lovely views, and points of interest along the way. One or two streams cross the pathway in places.

Most of the walks in this book include views of the Wrekin from one aspect or another. Its eastern side (owned chiefly by Lord Forrester of Willey Hall) overlooks Telford and the Ironbridge Gorge whilst its western flanks (largely in the ownership of Lord Barnard's Raby Estate) look out on to the Severn Valley and the flatter landscape around Shrewsbury. On a clear day, the Wrekin's summit (not included in this walk) provides perhaps the most stunning panorama in the whole of the Midlands - literally mile upon mile of glorious scenery in all directions. It seems appropriate then, to include a walk on this hill's hallowed slopes themselves, and also supply at least some information about Shropshire's most famous hill. The Wrekin at 1335

feet (407 metres) is by no means Shropshire's tallest hill, but undoubtedly the best known. Other walks in the book will show that the Wrekin sits proudly atop a huge expanse of flowing landscape making it clearly visible to most parts of the large county of Shropshire and beyond. Such expressions as 'going all round the Wrekin' (to describe a loquacious talker) and 'all friends round the Wrekin' (a local toast) are well known throughout much of the county and elsewhere. In my childhood, and, of course, much earlier, it was the done thing for local families to climb the Wrekin in great numbers on Bank Holidays and enjoy a picnic and adventurous games on the summit. Despite folklore indicating the work of a disenchanted giant with a shovelful

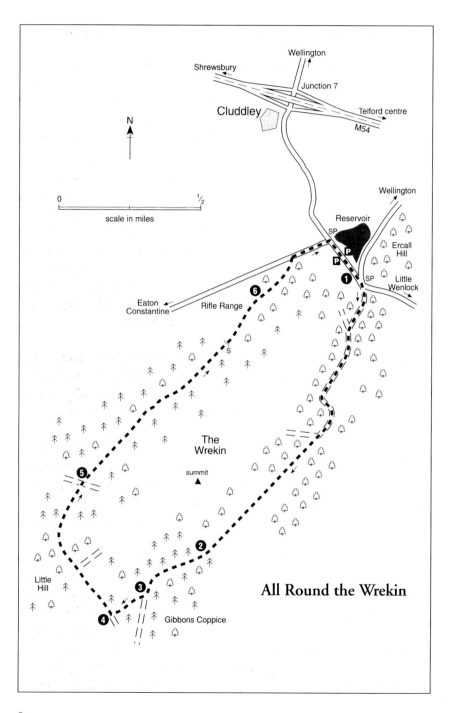

N

0   ½

scale in miles

Wellington

Shrewsbury

Junction 7

Telford centre

M54

Cluddley

Wellington

Reservoir

SP

P

P

Ercall
Hill

Little
Wenlock

❶

SP

Eaton
Constantine

Rifle Range

❻

S

The
Wrekin

summit
▲

❺

Little
Hill

❷

❸

❹

Gibbons Coppice

All Round the Wrekin

of earth, the origins of the hill lie in the volcanic activity of the late Precambrian period (roughly 600 million years ago). Not that the Wrekin was ever a volcano - faulting pushed the rocks to the earth's surface and it was left to the elements eventually to shape the Wrekin into the familiar hogs-back so well known today.

1. Park at the roadside and walk towards the nearby signpost to 'Little Wenlock' at a road junction. To the right stands a wide entrance leading to the broad track which takes you up the first part of the walk. There is a fairly steep climb for the first few hundred yards, with the consolation of some interesting views of the cliff-face and woodland of the Ercall Hill to the left. The pathway continues through mixed woodland of birch, oak and beech along the perimeter of the hill. Ignore the broad, steep trackway which climbs sharply to the right, this leads to the summit, and keep straight ahead. Where the main trackway veers upwards to the right, (leading to a rocky outcrop near the summit known as the 'Cuckoo Cup') carry straight on along a narrower path round the side of the hill. Ignore the metal gate down the left-hand side.

The immediate landscape on the left is a mixture of farm pasture land and deciduous woodland whose underlying rock is rather different to that of the Wrekin, and gives a softer shape to the scenery. Beyond the hillsides lies unseen the village of Little Wenlock, for many years the centre of an area of opencast coal mining. However, the village and its surrounding fields are now resettling into their pre-industrial attractiveness, and it is hoped that the countryside will soon become as picturesque as that which greets the walker's eye at this point in the walk.

2. The well-defined track takes you back into woodland then winds and occasionally climbs around the side of the hill.

There is somehow, an agreeable and secure feel about the walk through the Wrekin's woodland and this section is very much a case in point. Occasionally, gaps in the trees to the left allow rewarding views of nearby wooded hills and also, the more distant landscape. Variously, Brown Clee (Shropshire's tallest hill), the chimney of Ironbridge Power Station, the tree-clad slopes of Benthall Edge and the lush countryside surrounding Wenlock Edge can be seen in the distance. In spring and summer the immediate woodland is alive with a diversity of birdsong.

3. At a fork in the track, bear right, soon passing pine-trees on the right. The path has now entered land belonging to the Raby Estate. There is traditional access to the woodland path.

Wenlock Edge and the razor-edged Titterstone Clee lie silently in the distance to the left.

4. At the T-junction, turn right, soon passing a single pine tree. At the next junction - at a small clearing in the woodland - take the left-hand trackway leading

initially between beech trees. Fairly soon the track climbs up to a more open area at the foot of the hill, with young conifers growing on the right.

The main woodland walk is now behind you and you have also passed through the border between the Wrekin and the Little Hill - a tree-covered hillock standing almost like a small off-spring of the Wrekin on its south-western edge. Close at hand to the right, the extensive bulk of the Wrekin itself lies proudly above, like a lion surveying its territory.

The path climbs again, towards a group of more mature pine-trees

on the left. There are views of the long, low ridge of Hawkstone Hill in North Shropshire, through a gap in the trees.

At this point, the path has shaken itself free of tree cover, so that the dramatic landscape of North West Shropshire lies exposed to the eye. Shrewsbury's flat topped, Haughmond Hill, and beyond it, the long wooded-ridge of Nesscliffe, backed by the vast expanses of the Berwyn Mountains and Vale of Llangollen combine with views of nearby Overley Hill and the flat farmland towards Shrewsbury.

5. At a cross roads, go straight ahead. Soon, the track approaches the now defunct Wrekin Rifle Range. Climb the stile ahead of you, and you will be greeted by views over Wellington and the North Shropshire plain. Walk virtually straight ahead, with the remnants of the range to the right.

The Rifle Range was first used during the 1914/18 War to provide soldiers with essential target-practice.

6. The path runs between trees once again. Stay on the main track as it descends through a clearing and on to a metalled lane after passing beneath a tall, metal 'goalpost' structure. Turn right along the lane with the Wrekin on the right. Walk for a few hundred yards to a T-junction. Turn right, sign-post 'The Wrekin, Little Wenlock', and in a short distance, arrive at the roadside verge where the walk commenced.

Drummery Lane - Wrockwardine - Leaton - Wrockwardine - Drummery Lane

O.S. Map 1:50,000 Sheet 127 Starting Point: GR 630 107.
When travelling from Wellington on the B5061 towards Atcham and Shrewsbury turn right signposted Wrockwardine and park at the roadside where the road widens soon after making the turn. This is the beginning of Drummery Lane. Distance: 3 miles.

An easy walk comprising fairly quiet, country lanes and field paths including a short stretch of the Shropshire Way. There are attractive views in places and the historic village of Wrockwardine is explored.

Despite the incessant roar of traffic along the nearby M54/A5 road, Drummery Lane soon leads the walker through restful countryside towards the slumbering village of Wrockwardine, with the reassurance that not all things are subject to change in this hectic world.

1. Proceed along Drummery Lane in the direction of Wrockwardine.

Soon the lane is enveloped in gently rolling countryside. A patch of woodland across the fields to the right indicates the centre of the Orleton estate which owns much of the surrounding land. Orleton Hall lies hidden amongst the trees on the right and is a large, attractive, white house of Georgian appearance although containing components from earlier periods. Part of a medieval gatehouse still stands but

Drummery Lane

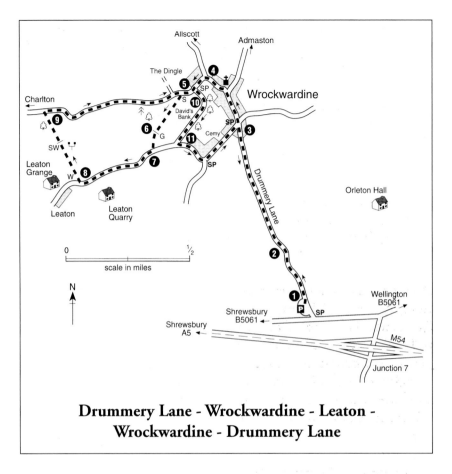

Drummery Lane - Wrockwardine - Leaton - Wrockwardine - Drummery Lane

it is believed that a manor existed at Orleton during Norman, and perhaps even Saxon times. In more recent times, the property has been owned by the Earls of Powis. If you turn around at this point, there is a remarkably close view of the Wrekin and its smaller neighbour, the Ercall. In summer the nearby hedgerows are decorated with honeysuckle, blackberry and elderflower.

2. The lane twists, then climbs and occasionally narrows (beware of traffic) on its three-quarters of a mile - journey to Wrockwardine.

One small clump of trees beyond the fields to the right represents the site of the lost village of Nash. Nothing more than a few mounds remains of this tiny settlement which may well have been abandoned following the Black

Death during the fourteenth century. On reaching the top of a hill, you will see the outskirts of Wellington in the distance to the right, and houses at Wrockwardine ahead, with Haughmond Hill providing an attractive backdrop.

3. The lane reaches a T-junction near 'Abberton' bungalow. Turn right then bear left towards the village centre (sign-post 'Admaston, Allscott').

Wrockwardine, so close to Telford still retains an air of peaceful detachment. No longer surrounded by medieval woodland, it nevertheless seems still to be in touch with events of bygone days. The first building on the left is the former almshouses built in 1841 in memory of Edward Cludde, a former resident of Orleton Hall. A memorial stone set in the wall reveals that Cludde endowed the almshouses (now a private residence) 'for the maintenance of two poor widows in their declining years'. Wrockwardine's real character lies in the cluster of mature country houses and charming cottages grouped around and beyond the ancient Church of St. Peter. An old Victorian Boys School is now a private house. The church is essentially Norman and has a magnificent tower, square and solid, with a short, brick steeple. Inside, there is an ancient font whose bowl is probably Saxon, and a Norman chancel window contains a copy of the Holman Hunt work 'Light of the World'. Wrockwardine (whose name derives from the word 'Wrekin') could well have been the most important settlement in the area in the days of Anglo-Saxon rule. It was also the hub of the Hundred of Recordine following the Norman Conquest.

Continue walking straight ahead and through the village, initially following the sign-post 'Allscott, Charlton'.

4. Shortly after passing 'The Coach House', turn left - signpost 'Leaton, Charlton'.

The Almshouses

To the right can be seen delightful views of the open countryside of the Weald Moors. Soon, you pass an attractive, brick farmhouse, clad in summer with climbing roses of yellow, red and pink on the right.

5. Follow the sign-post 'Charlton' for a short distance only. In a few yards, cross a stile into a field on the left.

The slight rise in the land is David's Bank. There are one or two outcrops of volcanic rock on the Wrekin's periphery of which David's Bank may be one. The summits of the Ercall and Wrekin Hills loom above the landscape to the left. To the right, the countryside falls gently away and soon there are views stretching way beyond the nearby sugar beet factory at Allscott, over flat meadows and softly undulating fields, to the long ridges of Haughmond and Hawkstone hills. In the distance ahead, as if determined to introduce an incongruous note, stand the buildings of Leaton Quarry. As the walk continues, however, there are ever-widening views over miles of surrounding countryside, with the West Shropshire hills of Earl's Hill and the Stiperstones joining in the rural pageant. In early Summer, foxgloves

and wild roses clothe the nearby hedgerows.

6. Follow the field path through a gateway into the next field. The path soon curves to the left towards a metalled lane.

7. Turn right and walk along the lane for about a quarter of a mile.

Soon, the western slopes of the Wrekin dominate the scene across the fields to the left. A little further down the lane can be seen a grassy bank on the right which, in summer houses a veritable 'cocktail' of wild flowers, including white and Pink Campion, wild briar rose, blackberry, yellow ragwort, greater stitchwort, poppy, blue bugle, and cow parsley. During week-days, the noise from Leaton Quarry increases as the walk progresses.

8. As the quarry buildings, and also the Wrekin appear through a gap to the left, and Grange House and other dwellings lie ahead, be careful to look for an opening in the hedge to the right a short distance after the lane curves to the right. Follow a way-marked signpost containing the 'Shropshire Way' buzzard symbol, which leads you to a path through the middle of a crop field.

The immediate view ahead left is dominated by Allscott Sugar Beet Factory. The fruits of many local fields are trundled to the factory by lorry during the Autumn months for processing at the giant plant.

The village of Allscott, about half a mile away, was once part of the huge manor of Wrockwardine. Thankfully, the main view ahead is of the attractive, distant landscape of North Shropshire.

Continue along the field-path towards an electricity pylon. The pathway passes the pylon and leads to a gap in the hedge. At the gap, climb a stile which bears the Buzzard sign. Walk straight ahead down the next field towards a large oak tree.

9. On reaching a metalled lane turn right. Stay on this lane as it travels the three-quarters of a mile towards Wrockwardine. Eventually, the lane climbs to the village. Soon after passing the driveway to The Dingle on the left, the lane goes past the stile to David's Bank and reaches a road junction.

10. Turn right, signpost 'Leaton'. The narrow lane runs mostly between trees.

Soon gaps appear between trees on the left, like the parting of curtains to reveal the tranquil tableau of meadow, ancient church, farm and country houses which personify the centre of Wrockwardine. It is worth mentioning also that, at dusk, or after dark the floodlit tower of St. Peter's lends a touch of melodrama to an already evocative scene.

11. At a T-junction, turn left. Pass a cottage on the left and then join a footpath taking you past a group of semi-detached houses. At the next road junction, follow the footpath round to the left. The path temporarily disappears as you pass the cemetery on the left. Shortly before reaching the signpost near the entrance to Wrockwardine village centre, turn right and once more pass Abberton bungalow then walk the three-quarters of a mile along Drummery Lane back to the starting point as the Wrekin looms ever larger ahead.

Cressage - Homer - Sheinton - Cressage

O.S. Map Landranger 126 and 127 Starting point: GR 592 041
By kind permission of the landlord, you can park at the far end
of the car park at the Eagles public house in the centre of Cressage, on the
A 458 Shrewsbury - Bridgnorth/Kidderminster road.
Distance: 6 miles

*A walk which has a bit of everything, field paths, farmland,
some delightful views, remote countryside, woodland, streams and
a country lane and village. There is a short optional addition to the walk
up a hill path for a spectacular view. The main walk also includes
a fairly steep climb up a long flight of steps.*

Present-day Cressage has to endure a busy, main road running through it. The village, which must simply flash by many a car window is not without its points of interest. Cressage still retains some attractive old buildings including a sprinkling of cottages along the main road. The name Cressage is thought to derive from an ancient word meaning 'Christ's Oak'. Around 600 AD Pope Gregory sent Augustine to Britain. One of his tasks was to meet a group of Welsh Christians (who had themselves converted a small number of Mercians) in order (unsuccessfully) to thrash out some points of difference in their respective ideas on religious observance. It is popularly believed that the meeting took place at Cressage - under a great oak situated where the War Memorial now stands, hence, the name 'Christ's Oak'. Today, the 'Lady Oak', duly fenced off and standing in a field alongside the main road on the Shrewsbury

Cressage Cottage

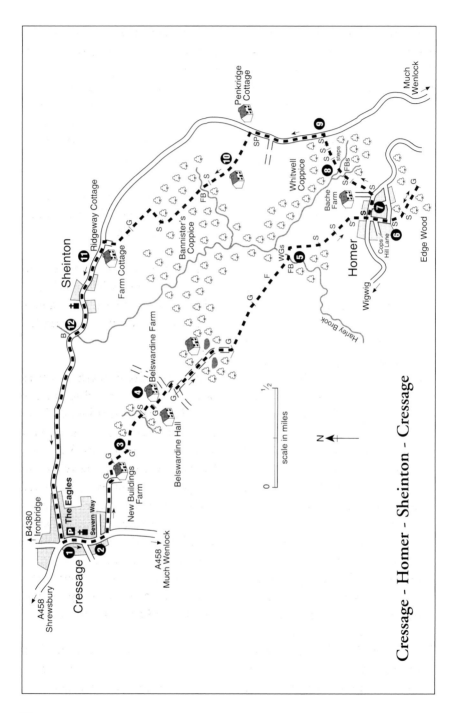

Cressage - Homer - Sheinton - Cressage

side of the village, is thought to be a descendant of the original. The tree died at an estimated 700 years of age in 1982, but new shoots have since sprung from its centre.

1. On leaving the Eagles car park, turn left along the pavement for about 300 yards in the direction of Much Wenlock (A458 Kidderminster road).

Soon, Christ Church is passed on the left-hand side. It was built in 1841 to replace the earlier Church of St Samson which had stood until then on a site nearer the river, but was vulnerable to flooding. On the right hand side, a pretty cottage, part black and white with a thatched roof and bearing the date of 1650, was once the village post office.

2. Continue past another black and white cottage and the entrance to Severn Way to a short stretch without a pavement. Just before a 40 mph speed restriction sign turn left into a metalled driveway passing a bungalow and some detached houses on the left. Soon, a distant view of the Wrekin appears on the left. The driveway continues towards a farm (New Buildings Farm) and bears right as it reaches the farm buildings. Immediately before the

farmhouse, turn left through a gateway and alongside farm buildings, before going through a second gate and into a field. Bear diagonally right across the field towards a gate at the far right-hand corner (ignore the left-hand, lower gate).

3. Go through the gate into the next field and initially walk along the left-hand side.

Curlew can sometimes be seen in this group of fields. The rooftop of a large, country house (Belswardine Hall) can be seen above a green hill ahead.

Pick up a field path leading downwards as if making for the hall. The path passes by two large trees and descends to a narrow stream in the valley bottom. Unfortunately, it is necessary to jump over the stream, but then look for a stile containing a yellow arrow on one of its posts. Climb the stile, and walk along the right-hand side of the grassy slope with a fence on your right. This will take you up to the buildings of Belswardine Farm.

Belswardine Hall hides itself from the public gaze and your earlier sighting of its rooftop is about all you will see of it. The house is said to have been built in 1542, though little remains of the original building bar two, big chimney breasts to the left and right of the front door. The infamous Judge Jeffreys once lived here.

4. On reaching the top of the slope, turn right, go round the left-hand side of the first building (a barn) then turn right towards the farmyard. Go through a wide, metal gate and between farm buildings. Turn immediately left across the yard and down an unmetalled roadway which bears right, alongside a brick wall before turning left (ignore the two gates straight ahead) and gently downwards. The roadway passes under a canopy of trees and by a lonely cottage on the left, as well as woodland pools on either side. Soon, you will be confronted by two broad metal gates ahead. Take the left-hand gate and join a narrow field path slightly to your left. Walk diagonally across the field, making for a gate at the far left-hand corner. Walk alongside a barbed-wire fence on the right-hand side of the next field. The scattered dwellings of Homer and the gentle swell of Wenlock Edge's eastern extremity can be seen across fields to the right. Climb a wooden fence and go straight down a fairly steep grassy slope towards a small footbridge over a stream at the foot of the valley.

5. Climb the wooden wicket on to the concrete footbridge. The waters of the broad Harley Brook drift slowly under a tangle of trees below as you cross the bridge before climbing a further wicket at the far end. Ascend a grassy slope, bearing right alongside trees. Join a narrow, field path which climbs between trees to the right. Ignore the wicket gate on the right but keep to the right-hand edge of the slope until a wide metal gate and stile are reached on the right. Climb the stile and enter a field, keeping a fence and hedge on your right. At end of the field, climb a further stile (yellow arrow) and walk through a small field before climbing another stile (yellow arrow). Pass by Edgewood bungalow on your left, climb a stile then join the metalled lane at Homer.

Homer has no church, shop or public-house and no real centre. It has one or two outlying farms and cottages but its main heartland consists chiefly of attractive modern bungalows and houses interspersed with one or two half-timbered and thatched cottages with lovely gardens. Its best feature is its location, perched on a ledge over-looking the Wrekin and the Severn Valley, and backed by the wooded slopes of Wenlock Edge. This is ideal walking country and at least one local resident has made it his business to preserve many of the pathways for the public to enjoy. He deserves our thanks.

6. A short detour can be made at this point. It involves a brief climb up a hillside path in order to take in the panoramic view from the top. After emerging onto the lane at Homer, cross over the road and into Cops Hill Lane. This quickly leads into Vineyard Road. At a left-hand bend in the road, look for a stile straight ahead (yellow arrow sign). Enter a narrow grassy track which climbs beneath trees towards the hillside. Near a wide, metal gate climb a stile and con-tinue along the path for about 100 yards, then bear left through a gap between the trees. Emerge on to an open hillside and continue climbing gradually, with woodland on your right. Make for a wooden gate at the top of

the grassy slope and then pause to enjoy the superb view.

You are standing where the long ridge of Wenlock Edge begins its lengthy journey towards Corvedale and Craven Arms. Immediately below you are the rooftops of Homer. Beyond, lies a vast expanse of varied countryside which includes a finger of dense woodland at Whitwell Coppice and the soft curves of the Severn Valley from Wroxeter to the beginnings of Ironbridge Gorge and Benthall Edge. In the background rolling fields swell upwards to the com-manding presence of the Wrekin.

Retrace your steps back to the lane near Edgewood Bungalow and turn right to take you further into the village.

Main Route Continued

7. After reaching the lane from Edgewood Bungalow turn left to take you further into the village. On reaching a grassy area on the left, turn left into the lane leading to Bache Farm, and almost immediately right onto a way-marked path over a stile in the hedge. Follow the direction of the yellow arrow as you set off across a field. There are cottages to the

left. Join the pathway alongside a wooden fence on the left and descend the slope towards a stretch of woodland (Whitwell Coppice). Climb a stile next to an overhanging lime tree. Descend a grassy track to the next stile and enter the woodland. Soon, cross a wooden walkway over a stream and go deeper into the woodland. Cross a larger walkway over a second stream, surrounded by lush vegetation.

You are now at the bottom of a thickly wooded valley where all is quiet, except for the sound of trickling and cascading water. It is a hauntingly beautiful woodland setting, secret and mysterious.

8. The way out of the valley is by means of locally named 'thirty nine steps' ahead. Actually, there are more than seventy brick steps leading up the steep flank of the valley. At the top of the slope, emerge from the canopy of trees and climb a stile. Follow the pathway keeping the woodland to the left. Climb three more stiles each leading into a small field. Walk along the left-hand side of each field until the path reaches a final stile leading to a metalled lane.

You have reached the country lane linking Cressage with Much Wenlock. Many years ago this would have been part of the main

Whitwell Coppice

thoroughfare between Shrewsbury and Bridgnorth.

9. Turn left onto the lane which is fairly quiet although you are likely to encounter some traffic. After about three-quarters of a mile, as the Wrekin comes into view ahead, the lane approaches Penkridge Cottage on the right. A few yards short of the cottage go through the signposted gap on the left and join a cart-track down the left-hand side of a field, alongside a hedge.

As you proceed, there are lovely views over the hedge to the distant hills of The Lawley and Caer Caradoc. Pheasant and partridge often frequent the field and hedgerow.

10. At the end of the field, go through a wide gap in the hedge and into the next field, walking towards the woodland ahead. Go straight ahead across the field cutting out its left-hand corner. Look for a wooden stile (partly hidden by overhanging trees) at the entrance to Bannister's Coppice. Climb the stile and pick up the woodland path which initially goes through a group of pine trees and leads down to a small, wooden footbridge over a stream and through the woods. The winding path soon climbs through deciduous woodland and (in summer) between tall bracken.

At the woodland edge, the path bears slightly left and over a stile at the entrance to a field. Turn right walking along the field boundary, keeping the woodland to your right. Follow the field edge as it turns left. Make for a wide, metal gate at the end of the field. You will soon see a brick cottage ahead as you walk along the right-hand edge of the next field. Just before the brick cottage, turn right on to a broad, farm trackway. This leads downwards to a metalled lane. Turn left on to the lane.

Immediately left, stands a small, cottage which was once a toll-house and by an Act of Parliament of 1778, became the Turnpike.

11. The road descends to the hamlet of Sheinton.

Sheinton is but a haphazard sprinkling of buildings in a crook of the rolling Sheinton Lane. The small church of St Peter and St Paul immediately catches the eye standing loftily at the summit of its own green bank, festooned with snowdrops in late winter. The Church is built of stone in the Decorated Style and has an attractive, black and white wooden belfry containing three bells. It was restored in 1854 and externally, little except for the tower and the west door (thought to have once belonged to nearby Buildwas Abbey) pre-date the eighteenth century. Inside, there is a two foot long fourteenth century effigy of a young girl. The Victorian village school was build in 1845 and is now a private residence. Nearby fields are thought to be some of the last in Shropshire to have been converted by Act of Parliament from open-fields to enclosed land, in 1813.

12. From Sheinton, the lane twists and turns for just over a mile to Cressage. It crosses the broad Harley Brook by means of a narrow, three-arched brick bridge, and a further stream before reaching the outskirts of Cressage. At the crossroads near the War Memorial, turn left and in a few yards, arrive back at the Eagles car park.

Great Bolas - Little Bolas - Cold Hatton - Bolas Bridge - Hunter's Bridge - Great Bolas

O.S. Map Landranger Sheet No. 127 Starting Point: GR 648 214
Centre of Great Bolas Village. Parking at lay-by, near telephone box.
Distance: 3 miles or 5½ miles

A fairly easy walk mostly along field paths, riverside and the occasional country lane.

Great Bolas and Cold Hatton lie amongst the rich and gentle farmland to the north of Wellington. They are surrounded by remote countryside as charming as it is aloof. Each of these quiet unspoilt villages has interesting tales to tell. Also, the character of the region with its sandstone cottages, old mill house, and changeless secluded countryside pierced by narrow, twisting little rivers seems to speak of a land where nursery rhymes could have been born, or fairy tales created. In fact, a true fairy tale did take place in Great Bolas during the late eighteenth century, and we shall learn something of this during the second part of the walk.

1. From the telephone box walk about 75 yards passing some cottages on the left. Turn left signposted 'Eaton-on-Tern, Childs Ercall, Little Bolas'. After a row of houses called 'The Meadows' on the left, look for and climb a stile leading into a field. The right of way goes diagonally across two open crop-fields towards a small, lattice-work bridge over the River Tern on the far, left-hand side.

2. Before the bridge there is a stile to climb near the top left-hand corner of the field taking you

Great Bolas Church

25

Great Bolas - Little Bolas - Cold Hatton - Bolas Bridge - Hunter's Bridge - Great Bolas

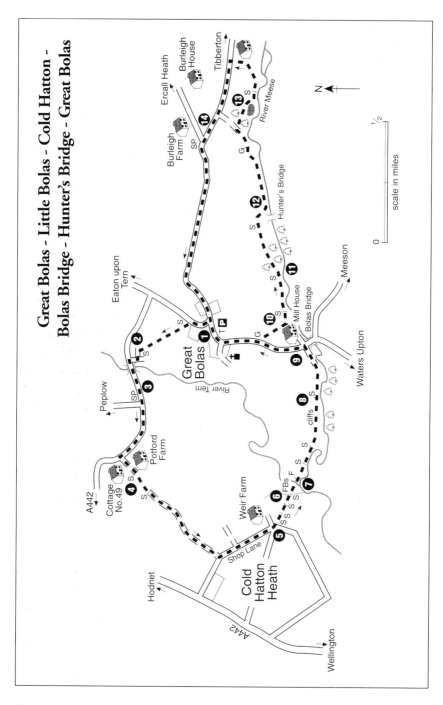

onto a short, broad track. The track soon reaches a metalled lane on to which you turn left and onto the bridge.

The peaceful scene from the bridge includes the narrow River Tern meandering languidly between cropfields.

3. Continue along the lane, past the signpost to 'Peplow and Hodnet' at Little Bolas, for roughly half a mile. Turn left immediately before cottage number 49, and walk along the drive towards Potford Farm.

The drive passes over Potford Brook which later wriggles its way through fields to join the River Tern near its confluence with the River Meese at Nobridge. There was once a ford crossing the stream near the farm, hence the name Potford. Potford Farm house is, in fact the final property of the Duke of Sutherland estate in this part of the world. Thus, cottage number 49, encountered near the beginning of the farm drive, marks the edge of his territory.

4. Pass the farm which is on your left-hand side, cross a stile and enter a field, keeping a hedge, then a fence on your left. Cross

the next stile and join a grassy track. When the track opens out into a field, keep the hedge on your left. Continue walking between fields. A view of Hawkstone Hill appears to the far right, whilst the dwellings of Cold Hatton come into sight ahead. The track develops into a wide, unmetalled lane, and at a T-junction, turn left onto Shop Lane at Cold Hatton Heath. Walk along the lane for about a quarter of a mile.

5. Just beyond a road junction and by the sign for Weir Farm look for a stile on the left. Go straight across a small field to the next stile. Cross the next field, keeping the fence to your right. At the field end, cross the stile on the right.

6. After about 15 yards, cross the stile on the left-hand side and then a small wooden bridge over Potford Brook. Go straight ahead, making for a larger bridge.

The bridge spans the River Tern about a mile downstream of the earlier crossing near Little Bolas. Oddly, this crossing point is known as Nobridge and it is thought that the name derives from times past when this important thoroughfare

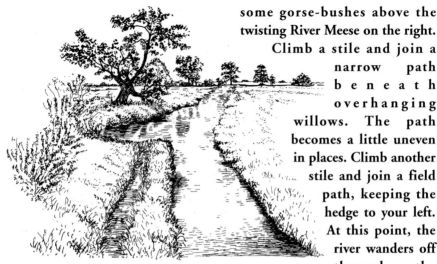

Confluence of the Rivers Tern and Meese

some gorse-bushes above the twisting River Meese on the right. Climb a stile and join a narrow path beneath overhanging willows. The path becomes a little uneven in places. Climb another stile and join a field path, keeping the hedge to your left. At this point, the river wanders off through the meadows in looping fashion, leaving the walker to pursue the field path. Soon the path climbs slightly and runs beneath tall, sandstone crags up to the left.

had no bridge but merely a ford. Horses simply had to trudge through the swiftly-moving waters, often pulling loads of sandstone rock for building materials. Several yards further downstream, the Tern is joined on its left-hand side by the little River Meese which has emerged from thick woodland and somewhat reluctantly snaked its way through the meadows to finally lose its identity within a now broader Tern. The Tern then continues to slide effortlessly through undisturbed meadows and fields en route for its own destiny - The Severn at Atcham.

7. Soon after crossing the bridge, climb a wooden fence and enter the next field. Walk alongside

The Sandstone outcrop is known as 'Cliff Rock'. Many years ago, sandstone was quarried here and transported by horse-drawn wagons, across the ford at Nobridge and on to Cold Hatton and beyond. Practically opposite 'Cliff Rock' and on the far side of the river, is a small island believed to have been a heronry at one time. The site played a part in the intriguing, but true fairy tale of Great Bolas in the late eighteenth century since it was probably frequented by a couple whose love story still fascinates people in the present day:

In June, 1789 a stranger calling himself John Jones joined Great Bolas society claiming he had come to study Shropshire antiquities. Sarah Hoggins, the lovely sixteen year old daughter of a local Miller developed an infatuation for Jones whose anecdotes of famous people and places gave her a glimpse of life beyond the confines of Great Bolas. After a brief dalliance with a middle-aged spinster at Meeson, Jones began labouring work with Tom Hoggins who also ran a small farm. Romance with Sarah blossomed and Jones bought a piece of land nearby on which to build a house, 'Bolas Villa', where he moved in February 1790.

When the subject of marriage arose neither Sarah nor Tom had any objections - the latter believing Jones to be a man of substance. Before marrying Sarah, Jones confessed to her that his real name was Henry Cecil M.P - and that he was already married! He had exiled himself, on his uncle's advice, to quietest Shropshire to escape the scandal of his wife Emma's bigamous marriage to her local curate in Worcestershire. On April 13th 1790, Henry and Sarah were bigamously married at Great Bolas Church. Cecil obtained a divorce from Emma and he married Sarah

properly in London; In Great Bolas Sarah gave birth to a son and daughter. In December 1794, Cecil's uncle died in Lincolnshire and Sarah's husband was to accede to his title of Earl of Exeter. The new Earl and his wife Sarah (now Countess of Exeter) moved to Burghley House, a superb Elizabethan edifice where the Shropshire country girl began to get used to an entirely new way of life, including mixing with Royalty and nobility. She bore two more sons but following the birth of her last child, Thomas (named after her father) she tragically died at the age of 24. Their eldest child, Sophie, is buried in the churchyard of St John the Baptist in Great Bolas, a seventeenth century brick building which also contains box pews thought to have come from a previous, fourteenth century church. There are more mementos of the Sarah Hoggins story should the walker take the longer of the two routes described.

8. Climb a stile and walk upwards between bushes, soon emerging into a crop field. Walk along the field-edge. The river is down the wooded slope to the right. In a few hundred yards, look for and follow a narrow track on the right which runs alongside the left-hand

side of a hedge. Walk past a cottage on the left and onto a short stretch of metalled lane. At a T-junction briefly divert to the right to visit the nearby stone bridge over the River Meese.

The attractive old bridge, which has a 20 foot span arch was built by Richard Madeley in 1795 after a plan by Thomas Telford. The structure contains a four inch covering of puddle clay to prevent water soaking through from the roadway and penetrating the joints of the arch. Wildfowl including mallard and swan can often be seen gliding along the waters beneath you. On the eastern side, an old mill house stands on the bank.

9. Retrace your steps back along the lane. To complete the three mile walk, stay on the lane for about half a mile as it climbs between fields then levels out before arriving back at Great Bolas and the telephone box.

Longer Route

If making the five mile walk, still head towards Great Bolas from Bolas Bridge, but after a few hundred yards go through a wide, metal gate on the right and into a field. Walk diagonally across the field so as to cut out the right-hand corner.

Near by you can see the rooftop of the mill house viewed earlier from Bolas Bridge. The house is now a private dwelling and the disused mill stands nearby. The mill was used to grind corn from the mid-eighteenth century until a fire in 1911. A paper mill occupied the site in 1665. The original course of the river ran past the mill house to drive an undershot waterwheel, whereas now it follows the path of the former overflow stream and therefore away from the house.

10. Continue along the field edge beside a hedge to the right. Look for a stile down a bank on the right. Climb the stile and follow the direction of the yellow arrow, diagonally across a meadow and then alongside the river which is on your right. The Meese has its source at Aqualate Mere just over the Staffordshire border, near Newport, and is little more than a stream until it reaches Howle and Tibberton, just a mile or two downstream of this point.

11. Climb a stile and go into a woodland copse for a short distance. Follow the path going to the left and enter a field, walking

along the field edge. The wood-land is now on your right. Follow the field edge as it curves to the left. Eventually reach a stile on the right. Enter a riverside meadow and immediately turn right and walk alongside a hedge on the right until reaching the river.

At the river you will see the remains of an old, sandstone bridge. This was locally known as 'Hunter's Bridge' as the hunt used to cross the river from Meeson Hall to reach the open countryside beyond.

12. Turn left and walk along the river bank. After a few hundred yards the path bears left, then right and passes through double metal gates. Follow a wide, farm track for about 75 yards as it veers left. Be careful then to turn right on to a partly concealed narrow path among trees on the right. The path takes you alongside an attractive pool on the right.

13. The path bears sharply to the right along the far edge of the pool with a fence on the left. Climb a stile on the left and enter a meadow near the riverside.

The path moves away from the river and there are reedbeds down the slope to the right, while the

bank on the left is smothered with gorse and broom. Soon after passing a group of willows on the right, the path climbs up to the left above the valley. Climb a stile on the left and follow the direction of the yellow arrow straight ahead across a field towards a cottage. Walk to the left-hand side of the cottage, then turn left on to a metalled lane.

Across the field to the right Burleigh House soon comes into view. Originally called 'Bolas Villa' this was the house built for John Jones in the Sarah Hoggins story. Even today, the sight of the elegant three-storey house evokes feelings of the romance and the oddity of Great Bolas's celebrated eighteenth century couple.

14. Further on Burleigh Farm comes into view to the right. At a road junction near The Old Lodge Cottage turn left (sign-post 'Great Bolas, Waters Upton') and contin-ue into the village.

A lovely white cottage stands to the left as you reach the turning to Eaton-on-Tern. The cottage was once the Fox and Hounds inn and it was here that John Jones first resided when he arrived at Great Bolas, long before living with Sarah Hoggin's family.

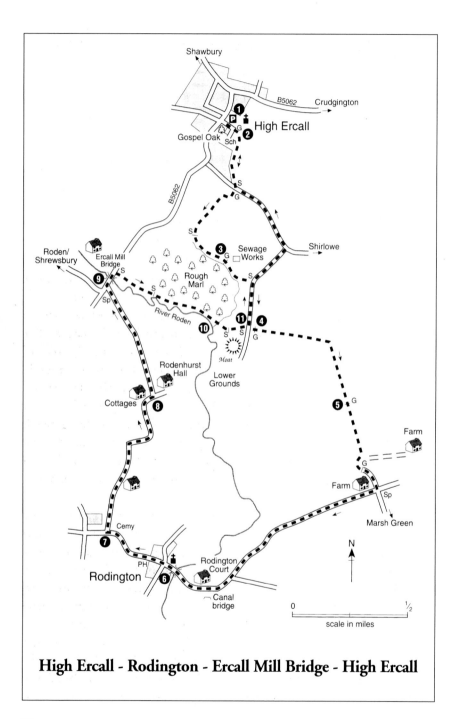

High Ercall - Rodington - Ercall Mill Bridge - High Ercall

High Ercall - Rodington - Ercall Mill Bridge - High Ercall

O.S. Map Landranger 126 Starting point: GR 593 174
Parking next to The Gospel Oak, Church Road, Near Church of St Michael,
High Ercall. Just off the B 5062 Shrewsbury - Newport Road.
Distance: 5 miles

A fairly easy walk along field edges and paths, including part of the Shropshire Way, and along quiet country lanes. The walk includes a lovely stretch of the River Roden.

There could hardly be a more historic beginning to a walk than the Gospel Oak at High Ercall. Although the monks no longer gather beneath its protective branches, the tree still stands in its attractive, grassy plot. The nearby, Norman church and seventeenth century Hall, together with the quaint almshouses on the other side of the village combine with a variety of mature cottages to ensure that modern High Ercall keeps a tangible link with its eventful past.

1. Park next to the Gospel Oak. Pass the 'cul-de-sac' sign and walk down a metalled lane with the church on your left.

The huge church tower was begun in Norman times and may even contain Saxon stonework. Cromwell's army has left its mark on the tower for all to see since High Ercall saw fierce hostility as one of the last Shropshire places to cling to the Royalist cause. The church contains an eighteenth century sundial, giving the time in High Ercall and also Jerusalem, Rome and Plymouth (New England). Next to the church stands High Ercall Hall, built in 1608 for Sir Francis Newport and later inhabited by the Earls of Bradford.

2. Continue along the lane and in a short distance turn right through a wooden gate. A grassy track passes the village school on the right. Climb a stile and cross the lane, then go through a metal gate into a field, following the Shropshire Way buzzard sign along the righthand edge of the field. A patch of woodland lies ahead. Climb a stile into the next

field and the path then skirts a hedge and veers left, passing the woodland known as 'Rough Marl' on the right.

3. At the field end, a wooden fence and metal gate give access to a trackway which goes past a sewage works on the left and a stream on the right before leading into a small field. Walk straight ahead, making for a stile at the opposite end of the field. Climb a stile and turn right, crossing a cattle-grid and walk along a metalled lane.

This short stretch of land passes through open farmland, with the attractive mass of Rough Marl wood to the right. As Lower Grounds farm comes into view ahead the distant views open out to reveal the flat topped length of Haughmond Hill to the right, and the hog's-back shape of the Wrekin to the left.

4. A few hundred yards <u>before</u> reaching Lower Grounds turn left leaving the lane and following the waymarked sign by a wooden fence. Go through a metal gate and into a field walking along the right-hand side of a tall hedge. At the field end, follow the waymark sign to the right and walk along

another field with a low hedge on your right.

There is a particularly good view of the Wrekin ahead at this point, and the nearby landscape is dotted with cottages.

5. At the field end, go through a wooden gate and follow the way-mark arrow directing you along the edge of the next field, keeping the hedge on your left. At a junction with the lane from a nearby farm on the left, bear right and walk along a field path for several yards, with a fence on your left-hand side. Look carefully for and follow a trackway on the left, go through a metal gate and follow a lane as it gently descends past a small barn and other farm buildings on the right before reaching crossroads. Turn right, signpost 'Rodington, Upton Magna'. Walk for one mile along this fairly quiet road towards Rodington.

Variously, there are views across fields to the Wrekin, Allscott Sugar Beet Factory, Haughmond Hill and High Ercall. Eventually, the scattered buildings of Rodington appear ahead, together with exciting views of hills around the distant Church Stretton. At the entrance to the village Rodington

The old canal bridge

6. Leaving the bridge, follow the lane as it climbs to the central part of the village.

The red-brick parish church with small steeple has a distinctly Victorian appearance yet the original building on this site was worthy of mention in the Domesday Book. Restorations during the eighteenth and nineteenth centuries have transformed its historic image entirely. The white-washed Bull's Head Inn is reckoned to be the second oldest public house in Shropshire and some of its out-buildings contain genuine half-timbering. Colliers from Oaken-gates and Ketley used to stay at the Bull for a week's cock-fighting. Perhaps even more grotesque is the fact that Bulls were tied to the school wall and baited with dogs. When the so-called sport was over, the hapless bulls would be slaughtered and roasted. To this day, there is a blackened inlet behind the retaining wall of the former school which represents the hearth where the roasting was carried out.

Court stands to the right. To the left, half-hidden beneath a canopy of trees, is a well-preserved brick canal bridge, a reminder of the days when the Shrewsbury canal was an important means of transporting goods to this and other parts of East Shropshire. The canal was last used in 1935 when twenty boats a day could have been seen. Rodington's situation above the banks of the River Roden presents the walker with a little vignette as pretty in its way, as some of the fashionable towns above the Loire in France, or Germany's Rhine Valley. Nowhere is this more appreciated than from the bridge over the river. The bridge was built in 1884 and includes stone from Grinshill Quarry and wrought-iron girders and lattice work made at Horsehay Works.

7. About one-hundred yards beyond the cemetery take a right

turn into a narrow, metalled lane. Stay on this farm lane for about three-quarters of a mile, passing a bungalow and a cottage on the right. At a right-hand bend Rodenhurst Hall comes into view ahead, across flat fields. At the next right-hand bend, pass some cottages before arriving at the farmyard of Rodenhurst Hall.

8. Turn left and walk alongside the farm outbuildings emerging on to a straight, broad driveway which takes you between open fields. The thick woodland of Rough Marl is to the right. In about half a mile, the drive reaches a junction with the B5062 road. Turn right, signpost 'High Ercall' and walk the short distance to Ercall Mill Bridge.

The bridge spans the River Roden as it curves its way around the old mill-house, now a whitewashed cottage. The bridge was built in 1915 to replace an earlier, brick structure.

9. Cross the bridge and walk, with care, along the road for a few yards before climbing a stile on the right taking you into a field with the river on your right. Climb a grassy hill ahead left. Soon, the river can be seen again on the right at the bottom of the slope. Make for the stile to the

right-hand side of the woodland. Bear right and walk for a while alongside the river.

This is a particularly idyllic stretch of riverside. In summer especially there is much wildlife to enjoy. You might see a dipper near the river, blue damsel-flies skim the water's surface and large fish hurry between clusters of white flowers within the river.

10. The path crosses a small stream and eventually climbs to a gate with stile. Climb the stile and follow the direction of the arrow leading you across a field and towards a further stile at the far end.

In another field to the right can be seen some quite extensive, tree-lined earthworks which appear to be the remains of an ancient moat. Lower Grounds farm stands at the far side of the earthworks.

11. Climb the stile and soon turn left into a lane encountered earlier in the walk. At a T-junction near Sherlowe Cottages, turn left and stay on this lane for about one mile. Look for the 'Shropshire Way' signpost on the right and thus follow in reverse the pathway used at the start of the walk, returning you to High Ercall church and the Gospel Oak.

Rushton - Charlton Hill - Eyton on Severn - Dryton - Longwood - Rushton

O.S. Map Landranger Sheet No. 127
Starting Point: GR 607 082 Rushton. Parking off road near the post box
at road junction (S.P. Charlton Hill, Donnington).
Just off Wellington - Eaton Constantine road. Distance: 5 miles or 7 miles.

*An easy walk along quiet lanes and field paths through open
countryside. There are spectacular views in the early part of the walk
over the Severn Valley, Wenlock Edge and the Stretton Hills. Small
villages and hamlets feature in the second half.*

Rushton is little more than a small, haphazard group of cottages, farms and houses surrounded by fields in the south western shadow of the Wrekin. There is some suggestion that Rushton and its neighbouring settlements were once part of an Anglo-Saxon estate connected to Wroxeter church, and perhaps even part of a Roman estate linked to the Roman city of Viroconium. One thing that is certain, is that Rushton's countryside possesses the oldest rock in Shropshire. There are a few slightly exposed sections of 700 million years-old rock (known to geologists as Rushton Schists) making Rushton's rock even older than that of the Wrekin.

1. Walk along the lane towards Charlton Hill, soon passing a tall, brick house on the right.

Continue past some cottages and the three Raby Estate farms known as Upper, Middle and Lower Farms on the left. Stay on the lane for about one mile.

In the early stages of this part of the walk, the slight swell of Overley Hill to the north of Wellington can be seen on the right. Between occasional gaps in the hedge on the left there are views of the twin humps of the Lawley and Caer Caradoc backed by the Longmynd above Church Stretton. Later, Wenlock Edge's long, wooded ridge joins the scene while the impressive bulk of the Wrekin looms large to the rear. As the walk progresses intermittent views of Haughmond Hill's flat summit, and the North Shropshire plateau of Hawkstone Hill present themselves to the right.

37

Rushton - Charlton Hill - Eyton on Severn - Dryton - Longwood - Rushton

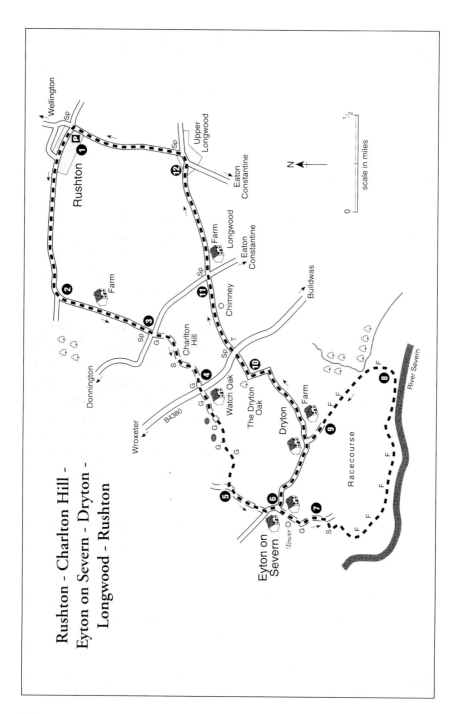

Eventually, the rounded peak of Brown Clee peers above Wenlock Edge on the left.

2. After about three-quarters of a mile, the lane curves fairly sharply to the left. Soon, a hedgeless field is reached on the right, with a patch of woodland at the far end. After a small cottage on the left, the lane reaches the edge of the plateau. The road then descends towards a grassy triangle.

At this point a glorious panoramic view stretches across the Severn valley to the Lawley, Caer Caradoc, Longmynd, Stiperstones, Earl's Hill and Pontesford Hill which stand silent and sublime across the West Shropshire horizon.

3. Follow the road straight ahead in the direction of a wide, metal gate. Go through the gate and walk towards the hillside. There is a large seventeenth century house across a small field to the right. The trackway soon becomes unmetalled as it progresses towards Charlton Hill. Stay on the path until it reaches a metal gate and stile ahead. Climb the stile and follow the broad trackway ahead as it gradually descends through the middle of a large field.

The descent from Charlton Hill reveals a thrilling panorama of unspoilt countryside stretching from the Ironbridge Gorge, and Wenlock Edge, through the Stretton Hills to west and north Shropshire and into Wales, in one magnificent, semi-circular sweep.

4. The trackway eventually curves to the right and leads to a metal gate. Climb the gate and carefully cross the B4380 Buildwas - Shrewsbury road, to a house known as The Watch Oak.

Near The Watch Oak is a milestone showing 'Shrewsbury 7, Ironbridge 6' a reminder of the days when stage coaches plied along this road. Before The Watch Oak was recently renovated it bore a plaque recording the fact that in bygone days a nearby oak-tree was used by a lookout to give advance warning of an approaching stage-coach.

Walk to the right of the house for a short distance, then pass through an old, wooden gate and onto a broad, grassy track between hedges. The buildings of Eyton can be seen in the distance ahead as the path narrows and then slopes downwards. At the bottom of the slope there is a small pool on the right. Go

through a metal gate and walk on the left-hand side of a field, keeping a hedge to your left. Pass by another pond on the right and keep walking alongside the hedge to a metal field gate near a row of small fruit trees. Go through the gate and into a field which is sometimes a mass of poppies in summer. Walk down the left-hand edge of the field, then join a pathway near a metal gate. Proceed ahead down the field path towards a small group of dwellings at Eyton, including the turret of a tower.

5. At a T-junction, turn left on to a fairly broad, grassy track between hedges and walk towards a farm ahead. At the next T-junction (with a barn on the right) turn left on to a metalled lane and into the settlement of Eyton-on-Severn.

Eyton stands on a slight swell in the landscape, and on its western side, below a strange 'pepper pot' tower (a remnant of the seventeenth century Hall) lie flat meadows beside the River Severn which in spring suddenly become Eyton's National Hunt racecourse. Spectators pay to stand on the grass bank between village and meadows to gain a view of the sporting activities. Eyton was the birthplace of Lord Herbert of Chirbury, a celebrated diplomat, philosopher, historian, and also close friend of Ben Jonson, during the Stuart period.

Eyton (Racecourse extension)
6. If making the extension walk over Eyton Racecourse turn right in to a lane and walk past a 'Private Road' sign towards an ornamental brick tower. Do not be put off by the sign since the local farmers have kindly given us permission not only to use the private road but also to walk the racecourse which traverses land farmed by them.

The Belvidere

The shapely tower or 'Belvidere', and a strand of ancient wall attached to it, are remnants of an old Hall at which Lord Herbert was born in the seventeenth century.

Pass by the left-hand side of the tower and then pass a cottage on the left. Near the bottom of the slope, walk along the left-hand side of a derelict cottage.

7. Immediately after the cottage turn right towards a wooden gate and old stile leading into a field. Turn left around a small barn, following the trackway. Enter a field and turn right, walking towards the racecourse fence.

For many years, National Hunt Racing has taken place at Eyton Racecourse on two Bank Holidays a year. Nowadays, the meets usually take place on Easter Monday and May Day Monday. It is difficult to imagine a lovelier setting for a sporting event.

Walk to the right of the fence and continue along the grassy race track.

After a short distance, pause for a moment to turn around and admire the view of a sandstone outcrop on a small, wooded hill. Nearby is a sloping, green field which provides a natural 'kop' from which punters can watch the progress of the horses.

Continue walking along the racecourse in an anti-clockwise direction as the course bends leftwards towards the next fence. Take the path to the right-hand side of the fence. Pass by the right hand side of the third fence and walk alongside a flat field on the right. The racecourse then passes through a wide gap in a hedge. Walk to the right-hand side of the fourth fence. After several hundred yards, the course turns sharply to the left and goes through another wide gap in a hedge.

For a fairly short distance, the course runs close to the River Severn which glides behind a hedge on the right on its way to Cressage and the Ironbridge Gorge.

8. The racecourse leaves the River by curving sharply left between hedges. You are now at the extremity of the Course which runs straight ahead for about one quarter of a mile with a low hedge on the left-hand side. Eventually, the course bends very sharply to the left once more. At the bend, pass by the left-hand side of the fifth fence. Walk along the left-

hand side of a stream which has a row of trees alongside. The stream disappears on the right. Walk on the left-hand side of a low hedge. There is a field, then a small, gorse-covered hill to the right. Walk to the left-hand side of fences six and seven.

9. In about 50 yards, turn right on to an often muddy farm track which emerges on to a metalled lane, opposite a cottage with gabled windows. Turn right onto the lane and you have now rejoined the main route from Eyton-on-Severn.

Shorter Route Continued

6. If not making the detour to the racecourse, pass by the drive leading to the Tower and continue along the lane. For a short distance there are tall hedge banks to the left and right. The lane curves to the left towards a black and white cottage. Continue up the hill, passing Upper Dryton farm on the right. At the top of the hill, the lane turns sharp left towards a huge, multi-trunked oak tree.

The tree is centuries old and locally known as the 'Dryton Oak'.

10. Immediately beyond the Dryton Oak, the lane turns sharp right and in a few hundred yards

meets a crossroads with the B4380 road. Cross the road and join the lane opposite (signpost 'Longwood, Wellington').

Somewhat incongruously, a square, brick chimney stack stands neglected in a field to the right, together with the remains of a kiln. The nineteenth century remnants of a small brickworks are reminders that the curvaceous local scenery has long sat on deposits of coal and clay. In the nineteenth century in particular, such resources were mined and used for the manufacture of bricks and tiles. Thankfully, nature is once again taking control.

11. The quiet lane continues to climb towards a farm near a road junction at Longwood. Go straight ahead over the junction (signpost 'Rushton') and past the farm.

12. At T-junction, turn left. Note that this lane can be somewhat busier than the quiet backwaters already encountered. Ignore the signpost to 'Garmston and Leighton', and stay on the main road as it curves left then continues towards Rushton. At a crossroads, turn left (signpost 'Charlton, Donnington') and walk the few yards to the starting point once again.

Lilleshall Hill - Lilleshall Village - The Incline - The Limekilns - Limekiln Lane - Lilleshall Hill

O.S. Map Sheet No. 127 Landranger
Starting Point: GR 727 155 Entrance to Lilleshall Hill,
just off A518 Wellington - Newport Road. Parking at Lay-by near entrance
to hill at end of St Michael's Close. Distance: 3 miles

The walk includes a relatively easy climb over Lilleshall Hill to admire superb views, easy walking along quiet country lanes, and a slightly tougher walk along field paths.

To the hurried traveller along the busy A518 road, Lilleshall Hill is a noticeably sudden lump in an otherwise flat landscape of agricultural fields, bearing a striking, stone obelisk on its summit. To the geologist, the small hill is the first real outcrop of volcanic rock at the north-east end of the Church Stretton fault. It is thus a relative of the nearby Ercall and Wrekin and the more distant hills of Stretton. It is a hill which easily reflects the changing seasons and, because of the obelisk, represents a focal point for the surrounding 'Duke of Sutherland empire'.

1. From the car park, take the pathway to the left of the metalled lane and walk towards the hill. The path soon levels out and the summit appears up to the right. Ignore the rather steep climb towards the rocky summit and continue along the pathway ahead which then climbs gradually. A convenient bench seat has been positioned allowing the walker to sit and gaze at the view below and beyond.

On the far side of the road, lie miles of the flat farmland of the 'weald moors' including Cheswell, Preston and Kynnersley. To the left stands the Wrekin and part of North Telford, while Longmynd and a chain of distant hills of South and West Shropshire adorn the horizon.

2. A short, steep diversion may be made to the right allowing the more energetic walker a closer look at the exposed rocks near the summit, and of course the obelisk.

The 70 foot monument, which can be seen for miles around, was built during the last century in memory of the first Duke of Sutherland who died in 1833. He is still revered today as the great landowner who drained the fertile fields and built distinctive cottages to house his tenants. The surrounding area is still dotted with Duke of Sutherland cottages.

If not making the diversion to the monument, go straight ahead from the bench seat as the path gradually climbs to a plateau. It is also possible to turn right at this point, using a less demanding route to the summit.

The views in all directions from the vicinity of the hill-top are magnificent. Beyond the village cricket field, the view to the east is more wooded and undulating, and includes two historic buildings. One is Lilleshall Abbey, of the twelfth century, badly damaged during the Civil War. The other, the mock-Tudor Lilleshall Hall, the former home of the Duke, emerges from the woodland as if determined to keep a constant eye on its surroundings, including Lilleshall village itself. The hall was built for the Duke in 1829 and is now a national sports centre. The view to the North from the plateau is of lush countryside leading to rural Staffordshire.

3. From the plateau, make the short descent to the start of a metalled lane. Cross the lane and follow the public footpath sign which leads down a narrow path between trees. Climb a stile leading into a playing field and walk diagonally left across the field making for a further stile in the fence to the left.

4. Climb the stile and turn right into a metalled lane which passes the village school on the right. Soon, a T-junction is reached. Turn right on to the main village thoroughfare. After about 200 yards you will arrive at the green. Immediately after the green turn left, following the signpost 'Old Farm Lane (The Incline ½ mile)'.

The Obelisk

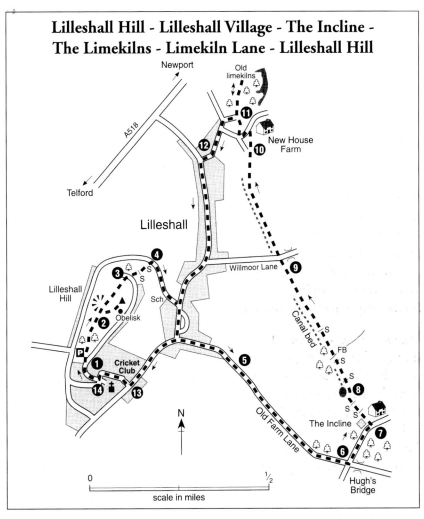

Lilleshall Hill - Lilleshall Village - The Incline - The Limekilns - Limekiln Lane - Lilleshall Hill

Newport

Old limekilns

A518

Telford

Lilleshall

Lilleshall Hill

Obelisk

Sch

Willmoor Lane

New House Farm

Canal bed

FB

S

S

S

Cricket Club

Old Farm Lane

The Incline

N

Hugh's Bridge

0   ½

scale in miles

5. The lane continues past a small tract of woodland on the left and climbs a short rise to a junction and a sign leading to 'The Incline' also to the left. The junction stands next to a small bridge called Hugh's Bridge.

The bridge once crossed the first canal to be built in Shropshire. Earl Gower, father of the first Duke of Sutherland had the canal built in the 1760's to transport coal from Donnington Wood mines to a roadside wharf at Pave Lane, near Newport. At Hugh's Bridge, a branch line went across fields to Lilleshall's limestone quarries. The dry remnant of the canal still worms its way through fields to the right and passes a couple of dwellings before disappearing under the bridge and into woodland. From Hugh's Bridge, the lane goes forward to become the Duke's Drive up to Lilleshall Hall.

6. Turn left at the junction before Hugh's Bridge and follow the lane towards 'The Incline'.

Wild flowers populate the woodland edge on the right in Summer, as the narrow roadway initially threads its way between trees, then passes by a stable which used to house the horses when they worked on the nearby inclined plane, long ago.

7. Be careful to turn left immediately after the stable. Follow yellow waymarker. Climb the stile and descend a peaceful, sloping sheep meadow to a pool.

You can see to your right the former inclined plane built in 1796 to replace a tunnel system, and along which canal boats were once horse-drawn to connect with the main canal encountered earlier. The pool at the bottom of the slope is, in fact a vestige of the canal branch line to the old lime quarries.

8. Turn right, keeping the pool on your left. The pathway leads to another stile. Follow a narrow pathway with a hawthorn hedge and fields on the right, and the dry track bed of the canal on the left. Climb another stile at the entrance to a short stretch of woodland. Cross a wooden footbridge and emerge from the woodland. Climb a further stile and follow the path ahead which passes between two open fields.

Where the path meets the Willmoor lane, a long disused brick bridge parapet hides amongst the vegetation. Its position shows that the branch canal used to run across the fields more or less along the line of the pathway just encountered.

9. Cross the lane and follow the narrow waymarked path ahead as it runs along the right-hand side of the canal bed which is very clearly defined at this point. Some of Lilleshall's houses can be seen beyond the field to the left, while gaps in the tall hedge to the right give views of gentle countryside and woodland. At a fork in the track, bear right alongside some farm buildings. Soon emerge onto a metalled drive near New House Farm.

10. Turn left, then after a few yards turn right on to a way-marked path into woodland.

The ravines to either side, are, in fact, overgrown lime quarries situated near the terminus of the branch canal. Over the years, nature has recolonised the area to provide a pleasant environment for the walker. Nearby are pools, rock faces and woodland now matured into a post-industrial state of beauty.

11. After several yards, turn left at a junction and descend a path for a few yards. Turn right onto another path between trees. After about 15 yards, arrive at the bottom of the slope.

Here stand four, brick arches, remains of the lime kilns built by Earl Gower (later Lord Stafford) about two hundred years ago. One of the kilns is actually beneath the first of the two slopes down which you have just descended.

Retrace your steps up the first slope and turn right along a wide, unmetalled track, leading to a T-junction. Turn left, virtually opposite 'The Barracks' and walk along a metalled lane, initially past a group of terraced bungalows. In a few hundred yards arrive at a T-junction with Lilleshall's main thoroughfare, Limekiln Lane.

12. Turn left. Further on cross over to the pavement on the right-hand side of the road. Lilleshall village extends for the best part of a mile along this road and the walk takes in about a third of its length. The road eventually passes the green once more and the entrance to Lilleshall Cricket Club.

13. Opposite the lych gate, turn right into a narrow lane which runs alongside the church wall and eventually reaches the junction with St Michael's Close near the Church.

The Church of St Michael is ancient and built in attractive red sandstone. There was possibly a Saxon Church on the Site and the present day building is of various periods. It has a Norman doorway and font. The nave is late Norman and there is a 13th century chancel. The interior also contains unusual seventeenth century memorials to landowner Richard Leveson and his wife.

14. Turn right into St Michael's Close, following the lane as it turns sharply to the right and back to the car park at the entrance to the hill path.

Coalbrookdale (Coke Hearth) - Strethill - Coke Hearth

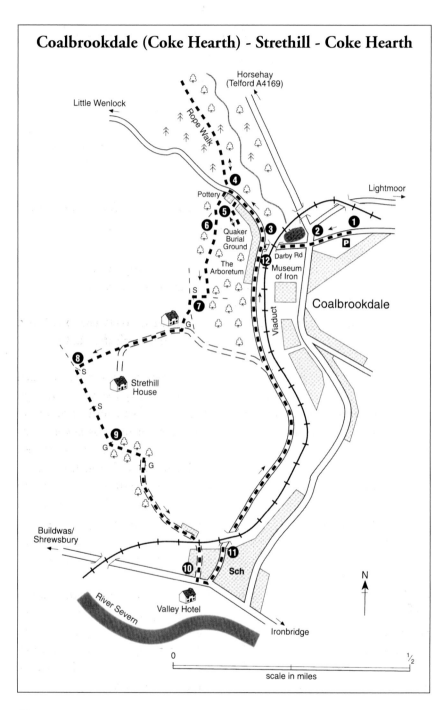

Horsehay
(Telford A4169)

Little Wenlock

Rope Walk

Lightmoor

Pottery

4

5

6

3

2

1

P

Quaker
Burial
Ground

Darby Rd

12

Museum
of Iron

The
Arboretum

Viaduct

Coalbrookdale

S

7

G

8

S

Strethill
House

S

9

G

G

Buildwas/
Shrewsbury

11

10

Sch

N

River Severn

Valley Hotel

Ironbridge

0   1/2

scale in miles

Coalbrookdale (Coke Hearth) - Strethill - Coke Hearth

O.S. Map Landranger 127 Starting Point: GR 669 049
Coke Hearth, Coalbrookdale, on the Horsehay - Coalbrookdale road.
Parking at quiet roadside area off main road opposite entrance to
Darby Road. Distance: 3 miles

A walk full of interest and scenic beauty which includes one or
two stiff climbs. There are echoes of Coalbrookdale's industrial past,
as well as woodland, field paths and quiet lanes.

Coalbrookdale is known as the 'birthplace of the Industrial Revolution'. Some superb monuments have been restored by the Ironbridge Gorge Museum Trust so that the area's history, importance and even way of life is being preserved for all to see. The walk will show us something of the dramatic scenery within which the events of the great revolution took place.

1. Cross the main road and enter Darby Road, walking towards a long brick viaduct ahead. Pass a pool on the right.

This is Upper Furnace Pool which used to supply water to Abraham Darby's furnaces. The complex to the left of the road is now the Museum of Iron and includes the very furnace in which Darby, in the seventeenth century first smelted

ironstone using coke, rather than the traditional charcoal.

2. Continue past the pool and walk underneath the viaduct.

The Victorian viaduct was opened in 1864 to carry the railway though this part of the dale. For many years, branch line passenger trains crossed the viaduct between Wellington and Craven Arms (until the late 1940's) and from Wellington to Much Wenlock (until the 1960's). Nowadays the line is used daily by heavy coal trains fuelling Buildwas Power Station.

3. Follow the road round to the right and join the footpath on the right as the road begins to climb fairly steeply. Walk past a footbridge on the right and continue climbing the hill.

The walk up the hill takes the visitor along an eighteenth century 'millionaire's row' of superb houses. Above a high wall Dale House looks down over the dale and the ironworks. It was built in the early eighteenth century for Abraham Darby I and is being restored by the museum. Next, Rosehill House has already been restored and furnished with possessions which belonged to the Darbys. The elegant house was built in the 1720's and mostly inhabited by the Darby family until 1908. Further up the hill The Chestnuts (now a private residence) is another impressive former Darby House. The Darby's, in true Quaker tradition, built nearby accommodation for the ironworks personnel. 'Tea Kettle Row' a terrace of cottages overlooking the large house is evidence of this altruistic philosophy. At the beginning of the row stands an impressive, light-brick house, Eastfield, which accommodated a manager of the ironworks.

The Chestnuts

4. Walk past the sign pointing to the Quaker Burial Ground and, after a few yards, turn right near a 'No Parking' sign and make for an iron gate. Go through the gate and follow the 'Buzzard' sign, walking along a path for a few hundred yards until it opens out at a meadow on the right.

The wall accompanying the path to this point used to mark the boundary of the old Sunniside Estate, land formerly owned by a branch of the Darby family. The open meadow is smothered in Early Purple Orchis during spring and early summer. This now idyllic spot was known as the 'Rope Walks' during Coalbrookdale's frenetic past, and the open space was daily occupied by workers stretching and twisting great lengths of hemp into rope strong enough to pull cages up and down mine shafts. Now, all is quiet, and nature has been swift to reclaim the ground.

Retrace your steps to the iron gate. Turn left, walking a few yards back to the Quaker Burial Ground sign and cross the road. Follow a further sign to the burial ground,

near The Pottery. Climb some steps near a large house, then turn right, going through an iron gate and into the burial ground.

Simple memorials to local Quakers lean against the two longest walls. On his death, Abraham Darby II bestowed a piece of land for such members of the Society of Friends who wished to be buried at the site. He was the first to be buried there although the graves themselves are unmarked. Rebecca Sorton Darby was the last of the Darbys to be buried here, although the burial ground is still used for cremation ashes. Some large, red pine trees are the only embellishments but the location and steepness of the slope

The Quaker Burial Ground

afford attractive views of the dale's surroundings.

5. Return from the burial ground to The Pottery and join a track which quickly climbs left into woodland. In a few yards, turn left again following the footpath sign into deeper woodland.

The woodland is known as the Arboretum and is now a semi-wild remnant of the Sunniside Estate. Within the tangled woodland are several specimens brought back to this country, mainly by female members of the Darby family, following their missionary visits to America to spread their Quaker beliefs.

6. Climb some steps taking you into the woodland proper. The path descends between trees, including a row of holly, and for a short while, becomes enveloped with overhanging branches. Go down some steps and at a T-junction, turn right. The path runs above a wooded ravine, then emerges from the woodland at a stile.

A sign near the stile informs us that the Dingle at the bottom of the ravine has probably been woodland since the last Ice Age, 15,000 years ago.

7. Climb the stile, then turn left and immediately right near a grassy triangle. Go through an iron gate and past a red-brick house on the left. 'Where the track-way reaches Strethill Lodge and the private entrance drive to Strethill House, be careful to leave the stone trackway by moving to the right and join a wide, grassy path.

Strethill House was built in 1883 for a Mr Squires, a director of the Coalbrookdale Company, and also a Quaker.

8. Climb a stile and turn left and climb another stile taking you on to a path which runs along the top of a green slope.

The slope tumbles away on the right towards the giant Ironbridge Power Station which dominates the scene at this point. However, to the right the soft landscape of the Severn Valley gives way to a broad swathe of fields and woodland stretching to the Stretton Hills, the Stiperstones, Cothercott Hill and Earl's Hill in West Shropshire. Not even the power station can detract from the unspoilt beauty of the distant views. What is now a tranquil field path over a hill top, was once a tramway carrying coal from the Little Wenlock mines across an embankment towards the Meadow Wharf by the Severn for trans-shipment down river. It is believed that the tramway also represented the first ever use of cast iron rails.

9. Go through a small gate and follow the pathway as it descends beneath a canopy of trees. Keep to the narrow track and go through a gate. The track eventually becomes a metalled lane. Cross the railway.

The descent through the woodland and the lane crossing the railway line were once part of an inclined plane carrying coal wagons down to the riverside for loading onto boats.

10. At a T-junction with the main Ironbridge-Shrewsbury road, (almost opposite the Valley Hotel) turn left, then almost immediately left again into Station Road.

The Valley Hotel was once known as Severn House and is the former residence of Arthur Maw, one of the great tile-making entrepreneurs of Jackfield.

11. In a few yards, the narrow lane passes by the rear of the

Coalbrookdale Church of England School, on the right.

From the earlier part of this century until the 1960's, this distinctive building was Coalbrookdale County High School. Towering above the school looms the heavily wooded Rotunda hill with brick houses and cottages perched crazily on its flanks. Beyond, lies the vast expanse of Benthall Edge and the Ironbridge Gorge.

The lane goes under a brick railway bridge then passes a sign to 'The Greenwood Trust' on the right before climbing steeply alongside woodland.

'The Greenwood Trust' provides instruction in crafts using coppiced wood so that the traditional skills can be passed on. The old station drive leads to the trust's base in the former Great Western Railway station buildings of Coalbrookdale. Across the dale through gaps in the trees to the right you will see the Coalbrookdale Evening Institute, now a hostel, where skilled artists such as those who hand-painted the fine, Coalport chinaware used to receive their instruction. To the left of the building stands the stylish Coalbrookdale Church, built by Abraham Darby III in 1851, and renowned for its peal of bells, including well-known hymn tunes. Immediately below, can be seen the Coalbrookdale Ironworks. At the bottom of the hill, the main entrance to the Museum of Iron stands to the right with rows of former workers' cottages opposite. Before 1890, the original coach road ran through what is now the Museum of Iron. However, Mr Squires of Strethill House, had the road diverted to its present route alongside the viaduct, whereas in earlier days, the cottage gardens, pig-sties and earthen toilets extended to where the viaduct now stands.

12. At the 'Give Way sign near the museum entrance, go straight ahead, with the viaduct on your right, and cottages on the left. At a T-junction, turn right, walk under the viaduct, and retrace your steps to your car at Coke Hearth.

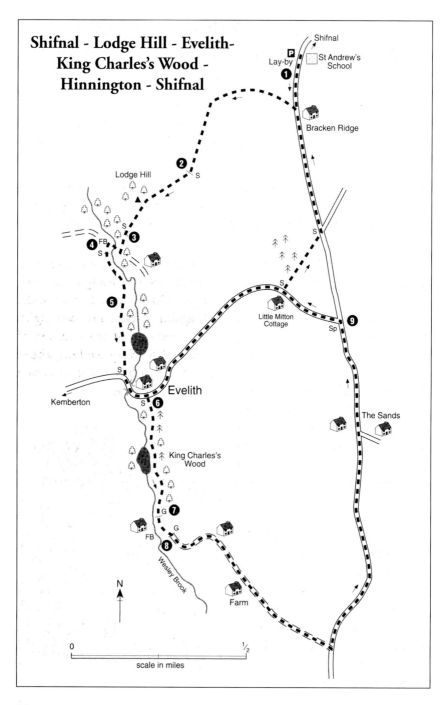

Shifnal - Lodge Hill - Evelith-
King Charles's Wood -
Hinnington - Shifnal

Shifnal

Lay-by

St Andrew's
School

Bracken Ridge

Lodge Hill

Kemberton

Evelith

Little Mitton
Cottage

Sp

The Sands

King Charles's
Wood

Farm

Wesley Brook

N

0   ½

scale in miles

Shifnal - Lodge Hill - Evelith Mill - King Charles's Wood - Hinnington - Shifnal

O.S. Map Landranger Sheet No. 127 Starting Point: GR 749 070
Off Shifnal - Beckbury Road near St Andrews School, Park Lane, Shifnal.
Parking at lay-by opposite St Andrews School. Distance: 3 miles or 4 miles

The east Shropshire town of Shifnal is surrounded by farmland and gently rolling hills. The walker's reward for getting off the beaten track in this area will be to experience the solitude and tranquil beauty of a locality often mistakenly ignored. There is history here too.

1. Walk along the lane leaving Shifnal behind. After a few hundred yards turn right opposite a bungalow named 'Bracken Ridge'. Follow the 'Public Footpath' sign along a path which soon approaches open countryside and curves to the left, while Shifnal lies to the right. The gentle ascent towards Lodge Hill now begins with distant views of wooded countryside surrounding the Wrekin's eastern face to the right.

The summit of Lodge Hill lies ahead, a knot of tall trees providing a natural crown. To the right stands Kemberton church. A few miles further west, by sharp contrast, can be seen the roofs of modern factory buildings at Halesfield, Telford. The summit of Brown Clee provides a backdrop to the scene.

2. Continue along the footpath ahead, with a hedge on your right. Climb a stile and walk alongside a fence on your right, soon arriving at the summit of Lodge Hill. Keep walking ahead along the path as it descends to a stile in the hedge.

Lodge Hill

3. Climb the stile and join a woodland track. In Spring, wild violets grow at the path-side. The path twists through woodland and reaches a stepped descent to the valley below. Turn right walking for a few yards to a footbridge over a stream.

4. Cross the footbridge and turn left following the path along the right-hand side of the stream. The path eventually climbs a grassy bank on the right.

5. At the top of the bank, the path leads into a field and continues along its left-hand edge before a picturesque cottage comes into view on the opposite side of the stream at Evelith Mill.

Beyond the cottage stands Evelith Mill House. This quiet secluded spot bore witness to events of English history during the extraordinary days of the Civil War. King Charles II passed by here during his escape following the Battle of Worcester. It seems he may well have taken refuge in the mill but was chased off by the miller and made his way to Madeley instead.

Continue along the path until a stile is reached leading to a lane. Climb the stile and turn left into the lane. Walk along the lane passing the impressive Evelith Mill House on the left.

The Shorter Route

Stay on this quiet lane for about three-quarters of a mile. On reaching the entrance drive to 'Little Mitton' cottage on the right, climb a stile opposite and follow the yellow arrow sign across a field towards a small pine wood. Walk diagonally left to a waymark sign near the entrance to the wood. Climb straight ahead and upwards through the pine wood. Emerge on to a field by a further waymark sign. Make for a stile at the top right-hand corner of the field, crossing the field diagonally right unless there are crops growing, in which case follow the left-hand edge of the field until the stile is reached. Climb the stile, descend some steps and turn left along a lane for several hundred yards until the starting point is reached on the left.

The Longer Route

6. Turn right and climb a stile virtually opposite Evelith Mill House, and walk along a track into woodland. The stream is on your right.

The woodland is still known as King Charles's wood, and reputed to be another part of the pathway along which the homeless monarch made his escape. In late Spring, clumps of yellow king cups cling to the water's edge and flag-iris rise out of the middle of the stream. A pair of Canada Geese annually raise a new brood here, and the surrounding woodland is awash with bluebells, white stitchwort, pink campion, celandine and flowering nettle, and alive with the sound of birdsong.

The pathway travels along the edge of the woodland with the stream down to the right. The path emerges into a clearing.

7. Go through a wooden gate on the left and follow the path uphill on the right-hand side of a hedge.

The stream runs through the valley below.

8. Go through another wooden gate leading to a farm track and walk towards a white cottage. Follow the farm drive as it curves past the cottage, then cuts between fields and a farm. A low hedge then accompanies the drive as it leads to a T-junction with a lane, near Hinnington. Turn left into the lane which leads through quiet countryside towards Shifnal. Walk for about a mile along the lane.

9. Turn left signposted 'Kemberton'. Opposite Little Mitton Cottage turn right and climb a stile into a field. For the remainder of the walk, follow instructions for the shorter route.

King Charles Wood

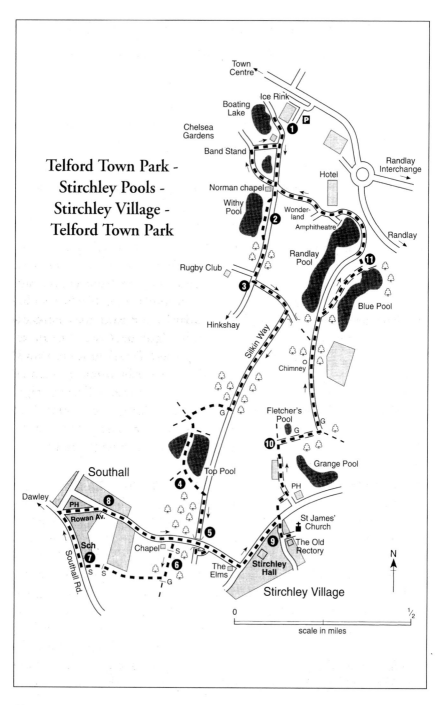

Telford Town Park -
Stirchley Pools -
Stirchley Village -
Telford Town Park

Town Centre

Ice Rink

Boating Lake

P

1

Chelsea Gardens

Band Stand

Randlay Interchange

Hotel

Norman chapel

Withy Pool

2

Wonder-land

Amphitheatre

Randlay

Randlay Pool

Rugby Club

3

11

Blue Pool

Hinkshay

Silkin Way

Chimney

G

Fletcher's Pool

G

10

G

Grange Pool

Southall

Top Pool

4

Dawley

PH

8

Rowan Av.

PH

G

Sch

Chapel

5

St James' Church

7

S

S

6

G

The Elms

9

The Old Rectory

Southall Rd.

Stirchley Hall

Stirchley Village

N

0   1/2

scale in miles

Telford Town Park - Stirchley Pools - Stirchley Village - Telford Town Park

O.S. Map Landranger - Sheet No 127
Starting Point: GR 699 085 Main entrance to Telford Ice-Rink,
Telford Town Centre.Various public car parks nearby. Distance: 3 miles

An easy walk along well-made pathways through the Town Park.
There are pools and woodland to enjoy, and some interesting glimpses
of a bygone way of life.

The master plan for Telford New Town included an open area, more or less at the heart of the town which was to be suitably landscaped as a large town park. This entailed preserving some of the semi-rural areas and former industrial sites around the old settlements of Dark Lane, Malinslee, Hinkshay and Stirchley, and welding the territory into one vast public amenity. Near the start of the walk are an ornamental lake, children's play areas, Chelsea Gardens, Wonderland and an amphitheatre. Further afield, the park takes on a wilder nature in which the combination of man-made pathways and natural regeneration amid remnants of early industrialism, create a surprisingly enjoyable and interesting environment for the walker.

1. Walk along the pathway from the Ice-rink main entrance, **keeping the boating lake and then Spout Farm House on your right. At Spout Farm House turn left towards some black, wooden bollards, and then turn immediately right past the 'European Regional Development Fund' sign towards open parkland ahead. Continue walking straight ahead along the metalled walkway, passing the small, Norman chapel on the right.**

For many years, the stone chapel stood neglected and forgotten in a field between the old villages of Malinslee and Dark Lane. In 1971, when a shoppers' carpark was being built at Telford Town Centre, the chapel was in the way and it was moved to its present site in the Town Park. It is believed to have been used as a lodging place by travellers through the ancient Wrekin Forest which once covered most of the area now known as Telford.

2. Make a short diversion to the right and enjoy the tranquility of Withy Pool. Return to the main walkway, walking straight ahead between trees.

The broad walkway was, in pre-Telford days a winding lane connecting the nearby village of Hinkshay and the town of Dawley with Dark Lane, and ultimately the main Wellington-Shifnal road.

3. Soon, look for and follow the 'Silkin Way' sign on the left. At the first junction, turn right. The path goes between open grassland and towards woodland ahead. Where the path emerges from the woodland turn right near two bench seats and walk past a wide, black, wooden gate, and on to a broad, unmetalled track. At a crossroads, turn left towards two pools. The track opens out into a car-parking area. Take the path between the two pools.

The pools are popular with anglers and the fairly short walk along the pathway has more the feel of a remote, country location than a piece of parkland. Nearby ran the western arm of the Shropshire

Canal which flowed from Donnington Wood to the river Severn at Coalport. The top pool was a feeder pool for the canal and the bottom pool was formed when the canal was breached due to mining subsidence. This is the same canal whose terminus can still be seen above the Hay Incline Plane at Blists Hill Museum, Madeley.

4. On reaching the end of the Top Pool which is on your right, follow the path round to the left and between trees (ignore other paths going into the woodland on the right). Go down a flight of five, broad steps, then almost immediately down four more steps, and turn right onto a metalled pathway.

The pathway runs along the track-bed of the former Wellington-Coalport branch railway line. It was built in 1860, and replaced one of the pioneering, eighteenth century canals, along whose bed it runs at this point. The London and North Western (later London, Midland and Scottish) Railway ran passenger trains, (locally known as the 'Stirchley Dodger') along the line serving such industrial communities as Hadley, Oakengates, Stirchley, Madeley and Coalport. Although much of that industry was in decline by the turn of the century, passenger traffic continued until the early 1950's. Small goods trains trundled along the line for several more years until 1959. The open area on the left is the site of the former goods yard which stood alongside the station's single platform.

5. **Walk under the railway bridge and leave the main trackway by means of a tarmac path on the left. The path climbs to a road (Stirchley Lane). Turn left onto the road and walk over the bridge. Turn left again immediately after the bridge and climb a stile, near a metal gate, taking you alongside a small, brick chapel.**

Stirchley Wesleyan Chapel was built in 1840 and originally served the mining community of Stirchley, a suburb of the town of Dawley. The chapel in the lane is still active even if its appearance seems a little incongruous, standing in a surviving patch of countryside amid an otherwise, encroaching urban environment.

6. **Join a well-made trackway which runs between trees. Just before reaching another metal gate, turn right along a further pathway between young trees. To the right, stands modern housing, while there is attractive woodland and a small pool on the left.**

The Old Railway Bridge

Climb a stile into the playing-field of Southall School.

7. Walk past the school which is on the right and leave the field by climbing a metal stile. Turn right on to a pavement alongside a main road, passing the 'Telford, Dawley' sign. Just before reaching the 'Queen's Arms' public house in Southall Road, turn right into Rowan Avenue.

Southall is on the south-eastern tip of Dawley, a town whose origins go back at least to Anglo-Saxon times. During the industrial revolution coal, ironstone and clay were extracted in large quantities to feed a multitude of furnaces, brickworks and forges. The town grew into a market town which also drew custom from the several, surrounding villages. In the early 1960's Dawley, which had for some years attracted overspill families from Birmingham, was designated a New Town by the government. By the latter part of that decade, Dawley New Town's brief existence terminated and the planners decided to go for a much larger entity encompassing virtually all the old towns of the Wrekin area as well as filling in the gaps between. Thus, the new town of Telford was born. The dialect and character, not to

say loveable eccentricity of Dawley's citizens are renowned and much of the old ethos still survives among Dawley's indigenous population.

8. At a 'No Entry' sign, turn right and follow the road into Stirchley Lane once again. Pass the chapel which is on the right, and cross the railway bridge. Continue ahead along a pavement then cross the road where the pavement ends and join another pavement which starts on the opposite side of the road. At the T-junction, with Stirchley road, turn left. Walk along the left-hand side of the road for a short distance. Cross the road to a pavement which passes a telephone exchange and the impressive Stirchley Hall.

Thought to have originated in Norman times, Stirchley manor was passed to Buildwas Abbey in the thirteenth century. Later owners included the Earl of Arundel. The present building was constructed in 1653 although parts of the earlier house are incorporated. In the nineteenth century, the Botfield family leased nearly five hundred acres of both the Stirchley Hall and Stirchley Grange estates to exploit the underground natural resources and establish colleries, ironworks and brickworks.

St. James' Church

the T-junction with the road. Cross the road at the T-junction and climb a short flight of stone steps leading to a pathway. Follow the path round to the right and it leads to a broad, green trackway. At a T-junction turn left along an unmetalled road leading to a row of old, brick cottages on the left.

The row of brick cottages, Northwood Terrace, was built by the Old Park Company in the nineteenth century to house its clerical workers. The houses were considered to be quite posh at the time since a good deal of Stirchley's housing consisted of low, damp and dimly lit hovels.

9. At the sign for 'Stirchley Spiritualist Church' turn right towards the Old Rectory. Turn left just in front of the rectory and enter the Churchyard of the redundant St James Church.

Built chiefly of Georgian red brick with a Norman stone chancel, it is the only church in Telford containing a significant amount of Norman stonework. The North aisle contains the family vault of the Botfields and there are other memorials to the family in the churchyard. The group of ancient buildings including Church and rectory represent the centre of the old village of Stirchley.

Retrace your steps from the church and rectory and back to

Follow a pathway ahead, passing the 'Town Park' sign on your left. A large chimney stack comes into view among trees on the right, as you reach a junction.

Down a grassy slope lies Fletcher's Pool whose predominant colour is red due to the presence of iron deposits in the soil. Here the Botfield family's Old Park Company blast furnaces produced iron near to the Shropshire Canal branch. Later, came chemical manufacture and brick-making.

10. At the junction turn right on to a broad pathway which soon passes by a black, wooden gate. At the next junction turn left and pass another black gate.

The well-preserved chimney on the left stands out like a beacon above the Town Park, a solitary monument to the hectic days of Victorian ironmaking. It was built by the Wellington Iron and Coal Company (the successors of the Botfield empire) but the furnaces were blown out in 1884. In 1886, Wrekin Chemical Company took over the former ironworks to produce a variety of industrial chemicals until closure in 1932. It is possible to inspect the inside of the stack.

Continue ahead (ignoring the pathway on the left) and turn right at the next junction. Go down the slope on the right to the Blue Pool and turn left along a path which runs along the left-hand side of the pool.

The Blue Pool is a restful place where thickening woodland clothes the clay mounds of earlier days. The tranquil scene hides the fact that much of Boulton's Randlay Brickworks now lies entombed beneath the deep waters of the pool. The works survived until the late 1960's, and its demise signalled the end of a frenetic era of industrial activity in and around this area, and the beginning of a return to nature.

11. Turn left across the grass and onto the broad, metalled pathway again.Follow the pathway as it passes near Randlay Pool which has the Town Park amphitheatre on its far bank. Continue keeping the pool left. At a T-junction, turn right passing 'Wonderland' on the left. At the top of the slope, turn left and the Ice-Rink comes into view in the distance to the right. The road curves to the right and returns you to the Norman Chapel encountered near the start of the walk. At a crossroads, follow the signpost to the Bandstand, Chelsea and Maxell Gardens. Pass Spout pool on the right, then the children's play area, and later the Chelsea Gardens on the left, near the Bandstand. Take the righthand path and walk back to the Ice-Rink entrance at the far side of the boating lake.

Ironbridge - Spout Lane - Benthall Hall - Benthall Edge - Ironbridge

O.S. Map Landranger Sheet No. 127 Starting Point: GR 673 034 The Iron Bridge.
Parking: Public Car Park or at roadside on far side of the Iron Bridge (ie. cross over
the river by means of the new free bridge and turn right and right again.
Distance : 3 miles

An interesting walk which includes some places of historical importance.
There is a steep climb at the beginning and also a fairly lengthy
descent of Benthall Edge Wood whose paths can be muddy and slippery
after wet weather.

The eighteenth century bridge provides an attractive and familiar starting point for a walk which takes you out of the gorge and eventually along field and woodland paths providing a peaceful contrast to the hubbub of Ironbridge's tourist attractions.

1. After enjoying the view from the bridge, turn your back on the town and walk past the Tollhouse at the far end of the bridge. Cross the road and the remnants of the former Severn Valley railway line and climb some brick steps immediately opposite, taking you alongside a large, brick house near the Station Hotel. Walk along a path towards some terraced gardens ahead.

Next to the white house down on the left can be seen some derelict, brick buildings and there is the constant sound of a stream rushing urgently towards the river. The buildings are all that survives of a once-busy cornmill and the huge waterwheel was once a familiar sight here until dismantled during the 1930's. Almost opposite the mill, on the far side of a nearby road lies the overgrown remains of an adit, a drift-mine in the side of the hill from which clay was once extracted for use at the local White Brickworks.

2. The path soon joins a footpath on the right alongside the steep hill which climbs out of the Ironbridge Gorge.

Originally, this was the main route from the gorge to Broseley and beyond, made possible by the

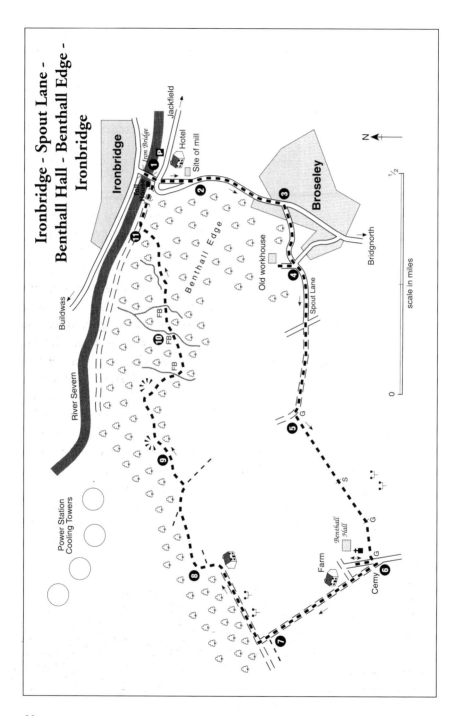

Ironbridge - Spout Lane -
Benthall Hall - Benthall Edge -
Ironbridge

opening of the Iron Bridge in 1781. Its precipitous - banks, now tree-smothered, were once the site of furnaces and mines.

3. Near the top of the hill, turn right into Spout Lane. The quiet lane eventually passes a cascade of water on the right which emerges from a metal pipe in the rock.

The spout used to provide the power for the Benthall Mill water-wheel.

4. At a junction with The Mines on the left, continue upwards along Spout Lane then look for and follow a turning on the right, indicated by a green 'Public Footpath' sign.

It is worth making a short detour at this point, in order to see the former Benthall Parish Workhouse. It ceased its intended function in 1837 and the part stone building has been converted into a private dwelling.

Return to Spout Lane. Turn right. At a crossroads go straight ahead along a broad trackway.

5. Go through a wooden gate on the left (yellow arrow)

and walk along a field path with a hedge on your right. At the end of the field, climb a stile and enter the next field, following the pathway. Go through a wicket gate and follow the pathway through another field. Continue along the path as it passes Benthall Hall on the right.

Benthall Hall was built in the 1580's by William de Benthall and was the centre of the old, medieval village of Benthall. In the fields at the rear of the house you can still see an example of the 'ridge and furrow' method of agriculture. The hall is currently occupied by Sir Philip Benthall, though in the care of the National Trust. One former owner was George Maw, the famous tile-maker. His great hobby was travelling the world in search of interesting plant species, which he brought back to Benthall. Some of them still survive in the Benthall garden including an abundance of crocuses. The church stands on the site of an earlier Saxon version

Benthall Hall

67

dedicated to St Brice. It was badly damaged during the Civil War and rebuilt in 1667 after the style of the original though dedicated to St Bartholomew. An interesting cast-iron gravehead lies flat on the ground near the church door. It bears a broken anchor motif and commemorates one Eustace Beard, Trowman who died in 1761, aged 61 years. Trows were boats which plied the River Severn carrying industrial cargoes.

6. Go through a gate and turn left along the metalled road for a few yards, then right on to a gravel trackway which takes you past a small cemetery on your left. Stay on the trackway as it passes by the left-hand side of a large farmhouse.

In 1645 a combined force of Roundheads made a surprise attack on the heavily garrisoned hall and nearby buildings. Part of the hall as well as the church and various outbuildings were damaged and in some cases destroyed. The small village of Benthall clustered round the hall was also razed to the ground. The village cottages were never rebuilt on their original site but at other locations nearer to the mines which were very active at that time. Thus, there is no village

of Benthall today - the peace of the fields has replaced the dreadful clamour of warfare.

7. Soon after the 'Shropshire Way' joins the trackway on the left, bear right at a junction and walk to the left of a metal gate. Enter a broad track with woodland on the left. On reaching a cottage on the right, turn left on to a path which goes into the woodland, initially passing between two small, over-grown quarries. Ignore the path to the right and walk straight ahead for about 50 yards to the woodland edge, overlooking the power station cooling towers.

You have entered Benthall Edge, once ancient woodland, subsequently mined and quarried from as early as the thirteenth century and especially in the eighteenth and nineteenth. It is now a delightful haven of regenerated trees and plants and home of a variety of wildlife.

8. Follow the path round to the right, with the cooling towers visible through the trees to the left. At a T-junction, turn right. At the next junction bear left, still walking with care along the edge of the wood.

9. Soon, the path reaches a fence on the left providing a good view overlooking the River Severn. Arrive at a wooden post bearing the figure 11 and an arrow pointing straight ahead. Follow the direction of the arrow as you join a stretch of the nature trail. The path descends then climbs, still running along the woodland edge. The wood is full of pathways but the basic rule from here on until reaching Ironbridge is to keep bearing left and descending through the woodland until the wide trackway at the bottom of the gradient is reached. Turn left and cross a footbridge over a stream. Turn right and climb some wooden steps. At the top of the steps turn left along a pathway through more woodland.

Apart from the mining of coal and clay, and the quarrying of limestone (into the twentieth century) coppicing of hazel and other trees took place over the years so that the wood could be used as fuel in the form of charcoal.

10. Cross a wooden walkway, then descend some steps. Cross a footbridge and climb a short flight of steps. Cross another footbridge over a stream. At a junction which has some steps on the right, bear left, descending alongside a stream which is on the left. Descend more steps, bear left then descend more flights of steps. Later, there is a wooden fence on the left. Bear right and descend a winding path and further steps. At this point, you may well hear the noise of Iron-bridge's traffic in the valley below.

11. The downward slope at last reaches a T-junction with a broad, level trackway. Turn right.

You are now walking along a short stretch of the track-bed of the old Severn Valley Railway which connected Shrewsbury with Worcester from Victorian times until the mid-twentieth century. As at this location, the railway hugged the river for most of its length, and the Ironbridge-Buildwas section saw the line pass through the gorge and below the wooded heights of Benthall Edge. The trackway passes over a brick arch (unseen) over the bed of an inclined plane which once carried limestone from Pattins Rock quarry on the Edge to a group of limekilns on the river bank. You then pass beneath a brick bridge which carried another inclined plane bearing clay for the 'White Brickworks at the riverside.

In a few yards you will arrive back at the Iron Bridge.

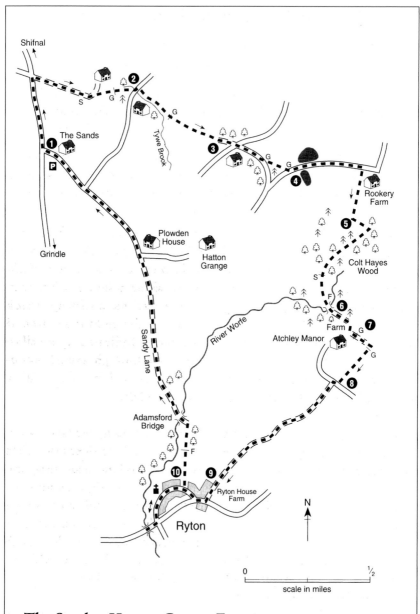

Shifnal

2

The Sands

1

P

Grindle

S

G

Tywe Brook

G

3

G

G

4

Rookery Farm

5

Colt Hayes Wood

S

F

6

Farm

7

G

G

Atchley Manor

8

Plowden House

Hatton Grange

Sandy Lane

River Worfe

Adamsford Bridge

F

10 **9**

Ryton House Farm

Ryton

N

0   ½

scale in miles

The Sands - Hatton Grange Estate -
Ryton - The Sands

The Sands - Hatton Grange Estate - Ryton - The Sands

O.S. Map Landranger Sheet No. 127 Starting Point: GR 753 048
The Sands - just off the Shifnal - Ryton Road. Parking at roadside near cottages.
Look for sign to 'Plowden House' and public footpath sign. Distance: 4 miles

A generally easy walk through the attractive farmland and woodland of Hatton Grange Estate. The walk also passes through part of the village of Ryton, and there is a short and fairly steep climb through Manor Wood.

The Cistercian Abbey of Buildwas near Ironbridge held a number of detached farms or 'granges' from whose lands grain was harvested to sustain the monks through the long months of winter. Hatton Grange, in the peaceful countryside south east of Shifnal, was one such provider comprising at its height some 1,100 acres of fertile land. The Grange has existed from at least the early thirteenth century. The present day estate is about one tenth the size of the original, and owned by the well-known Shropshire family, the Kenyon-Slaneys.

1. Walk the short distance back to the road and turn right. Walk along the fairly quiet road for one-quarter of a mile until a signpost for Kemberton. Turn right and follow a public footpath sign leading you along a wide trackway beside a cropfield, with a hedge on your right. Climb a stile next to a gateway. Walk ahead along a house drive, then join a narrow pathway which passes to the right-hand side of the house, indicated by a yellow arrow. Go through a small, wooden gate. At a T-junction with a lane, turn left.

2. In a few yards, the lane crosses Twye brook. Turn right into a field (follow the yellow arrow sign) and walk along its right-hand edge with the stream and woodland on your right. Go through the gateway which leads to a path through the middle of the next field and towards woodland ahead.

Beyond the fields to the left lie views of gently sloping countryside including the low, wooded Lizard Hill near Tong.

3. The trackway leads briefly alongside a patch of woodland, then on to a junction with a metalled lane.

Go straight across the junction and walk along a quiet lane with beech trees standing to the right. At a sharp right-hand bend in the lane, leave the road, go through a gate on your left and cross a field path, passing a small group of pine trees. Walk towards a gate at the far end of the field.

Nearby, though not visible to the walker, Hatton Grange, a lovely Georgian country house enjoys its privacy amongst woodland and beside stylish gardens. The grounds also include pretty dingles and pools thought to have originated from the grange's earlier monastic connection.

4. Go through the large, metal gate and turn left on to a metalled lane. Stay on the lane as it approaches Rookery Farm ahead. Immediately before reaching the farm buildings, turn right onto a wide trackway which runs along a field edge with the farm on your left. Continue along the path as it approaches woodland ahead.

Across fields to the left you will see the hangars of Cosford Aerodrome.

Once an ancient settlement near the border with rural Staffordshire, Cosford has long since become a 'Royal Airforce Village'. The aerospace museum and also a gliding club provide leisure amenities to members of the public.

5. On entering the next field, walk along its left-hand perimeter until arriving at the left-hand corner. Climb over a rough, wooden fence on the left and join a woodland track. After about 20 yards, turn right onto a further track with pine trees initially on the right-hand side.

You have entered Colt Hayes Wood. Bluebells enjoy the subdued light in late spring. A shallow valley runs below the woodland down to the left carrying the infant River Worfe towards Ryton and ultimately, its union with the Severn near Bridgnorth.

The track bears left and descends into mixed woodland before reaching a field gate to the left of a stile. Climb the stile whose yellow arrow direction is a little misleading. Ignore the grassy slope to the right and walk down the field towards more woodland, and a small bridge over the

Worfe. Make for a broad, metal gate with some wooden fencing on its left-hand side. Climb the fence and cross the bridge, entering the woodland.

The little river flowing under the bridge is The Worfe which begins life as an insignificant stream at Redhill near St. Georges, Telford. Pickmere Lake and Tong Forge feature on its itinerary before it enters the Hatton Grange Estate. The short walk through Manor Wood is enchanting.

6. Climb the track through the woodland. It bears right and then narrows as it passes between tall oak and pine. At the summit of the climb, the path emerges from the woodland and runs along the left-hand side of some farm buildings.

The farm is attached to Atchley Manor, another part of the Hatton Estate. The Manor hides behind the farm buildings and bears the year 1588 etched in sandstone on one of its walls.

7. Join a broad track still to the left of the farm buildings and with an open

field on the left. Go through, or if necessary climb a wide, metal gate and walk through a small field. At the end of the field turn right and go through another metal gate entering a much larger field, walking down its right-hand side, with a hedge on your right.

8. At the end of the field turn right briefly on to a metalled lane which goes to Atchley Manor. After a few yards turn left on to a wide, farm track. The track goes between open fields towards Ryton House Farm.

9. Pass some farm buildings on the right. At a T-junction turn right onto a metalled lane. Walk along the lane for a short distance then turn right (signpost 'Ryton

Church House

Church School'). You are now in the village of Ryton. If you do not wish to explore the village then immediately before Church House turn right and go through a gate into a field.

If you want to see what Ryton has to offer before continuing with the main walk, keep straight ahead towards the Church, passing some attractive cottages and houses. Despite the Victorian Gothic appearance of its exterior, St Andrew's church contains such features as an eighteenth century tower and chancel, a fourteenth century font, and stone work in two of its outer walls which could belong to the twelfth century. Continue down the hill to arrive at the little bridge over the Worfe. Retrace your steps back to the Church and eventually Church House.

10. Walk along the field path with Church House on your left. Arrive at a point where a metal gate stands next to some wooden fencing on its right. Climb the fence and join a narrow track leading downwards between bushes and overhanging trees. Ignore the field gate ahead and follow a broad trackway (Sandy Lane) leading to the left and across the shallow river at Adamsford Bridge. After three-quarters of a mile go straight ahead at a junction joining a metalled lane which takes you past Plowden House on the right.

Plowden House was once also known as 'Hatton Grange' and this inevitably led over the years to confusion with the main property on the estate. In 1969, the name was altered to Plowden House in memory of Plowden Slaney who had the other house built in the eighteenth century. Plowden House is the farmhouse to Grange Farm.

Soon you will arrive back at The Sands and the starting point of the walk.

Little Dawley - Gravel Leasowes - Lightmoor - Little Dawley

O.S. Map Landranger Sheet No. 127 Starting Point: GR 686 058
Castle Pools, Little Dawley. Parking at Castle Pools Car Park,
Off South View Road, Little Dawley. Distance: 3 miles

A fairly easy and often fascinating walk, mostly along pathways through sites of former industrial activity now recolonised by nature. There are also attractive pools and a woodland path down an old inclined plane.

This walk is entirely within the confines of Telford yet takes you through quiet, almost secret places which both echo the area's industrial past and reflect the semi-rural atmosphere which has characterised certain parts of the town for the best part of two hundred years.

1. From the car park turn left and immediately right on to a narrow pathway taking you to the left-hand side of a stretch of water. Follow the pathway along the water's edge.

On the far bank the dwellings of Little Dawley have gradually encroached to the water side. The now enlarged pool has been known for generations as the 'Wide Waters'. Peaceful now, it used to be part of

the narrow, Coalbrookdale Branch of the Shropshire Union Canal and was a turning point for barges.

2. The path continues ahead through woodland. A narrow stretch of water on the right-hand side is a remnant of the old canal, whilst dense woodland lies to the left. The woodland path soon opens out (this used to be a canal

Wide Waters

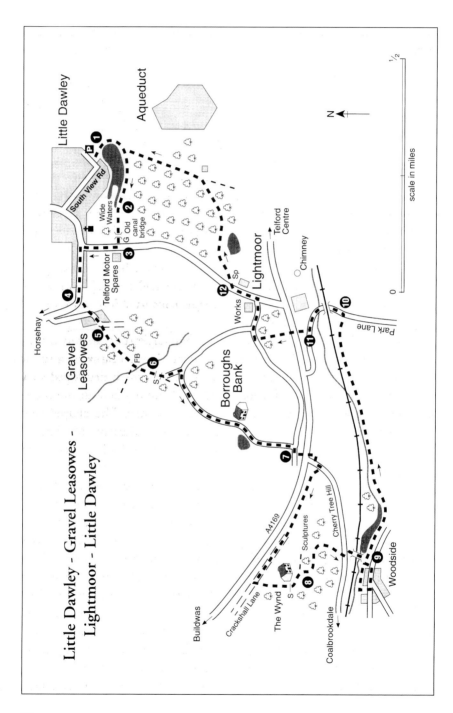

Little Dawley - Gravel Leasowes - Lightmoor - Little Dawley

Little Dawley

Aqueduct

South View Rd

Wide Waters

G Old canal bridge

Telford Motor Spares

Horsehay

Gravel Leasowes

FB

Borroughs Bank

Works

Lightmoor

Sp

Telford Centre

Chimney

Park Lane

A4169

Crackshall Lane

The Wynd

Sculptures

Buildwas

Cherry Tree Hill

Coalbrookdale

Woodside

N

scale in miles

0   ½

basin) and passes through a stone cutting and then under a brick bridge.

The bridge was restored in 1994. The canal once flowed beneath whilst a tramway passed over the top, carrying coal for loading on to canal boats.

3. Go through a wooden gate (opposite 'Telford Motor Spares') and turn right onto a metalled road climbing for about 75 yards to a road junction at Little Dawley. Turn left into Holly Road (Signpost 'Doseley, Horsehay) and walk down the road for a few hundred yards. The road passes a half-timbered cottage on the right, then descends between small fields and some former pit-mounds now tree covered.

One such mound on the right is known as Springwell Mound, the scene of a pit tragedy in the late eighteenth century when a rope gave way on the pit cage resulting in the deaths of eight miners. The bodies were laid out at the Crown Inn, a timber-framed building which used to stand near Little Dawley Chapel. It has in recent years, been moved to the Ironbridge Gorge Museum Site at Blists Hill where it is now the Estate Office.

4. At the bottom of the slope, the road curves sharply to the right but leave the road at this point and follow a narrow pathway to the left leading towards some cottages. The pathway crosses the trackbed of the former Great Western Railway branch line from Wellington to Craven Arms, now merely a narrow path. At a T-junction with a lane opposite a cottage, turn left and the lane soon becomes unmetalled as it approaches a further group of dwellings and a small, redundant chapel converted into a house.

You have arrived at the tiny settlement of Gravel Leasowes, a small community which developed as a result of mining here in the nineteenth century. The chapel was Lightmoor Primitive Methodist Jubilee Chapel, built in 1863 but closed around 1903. It was affectionately known as 'Pop Bottle' chapel - a reference to the cramped inside dimensions. Certainly its demise mirrors the decline of the area as mines became substantially worked out and populations moved elsewhere. For much of the twentieth century however, Gravel Leasowes has more or less survived as a tiny, close-knit community where generations of the same families have lived in small cottages in splendid isolation.

5. Take the path to the right immediately opposite the chapel and leading into a woodland copse. At a fork in the pathway, take the left-hand path which takes you across a narrow footbridge over a stream. Ignore stile and waymark and walk along a path on the other side, which climbs gradually up a field bank on the right-hand side of the stream.

The walk down to the stream has taken you over the 'Blackie Mount' a remnant of earlier coal-mining days, also the former site of a squatter cottage. The field path alongside the stream is known as 'The Wytcherley'.

6. Continue along the field path as it climbs between trees then levels out towards a stile ahead. Ignore stile and waymark on right. Climb stile and then turn right onto a broad trackway. At a junction at the top of the slope, turn left and descend a trackway which at first runs alongside a field and then some cottages and a pool.

You have arrived at another former small industrial settlement, known as Burroughs Bank. Red clay was mined here at the Ash Tree pit until 1908 and transported by tramway across fields to the Shutfield tile

works at nearby Lightmoor. Still visible just off the trackway are some weathering deposits of red clay, and the base of the old winding engine house. One of the Burroughs Bank's squatter cottages is now a working exhibit at Blists Hill museum, whilst others have been tastefully restored in situ.

7. At a T-junction, turn right for a few yards then be careful to turn left onto a narrow path leading to some steps. Go down the steps then cross the busy main road (the Ironbridge gorge by-pass) and turn right along a footpath which soon turns left into Cherry Tree Hill. After about

The Steps,
Cherry Tree Hill

75 yards cross the road and join a trackway opposite which climbs from the roadside and initially runs above the main road on the right. The path becomes a grassy trackway running between hedges. On arriving at the 'Crackshall Lane' sign, turn left at a broad, wooden gate marked 'The Old Wynd House' and walk along a wide track towards some cottages on the left.

This attractive wooded area would have been a hive of activity in the late eighteenth and nineteenth centuries. The canal reached a point at The Wynd where the land fell steeply towards the dale at Coalbrookdale. Tub boats laden with coal and iron-stone had to be lowered into the dale to feed Abraham Darby's furnaces. The hauliers briefly flirted with a tunnel and shaft system then settled for an inclined plane. The Wynd was thus a busy transit point for the transfer of tub boats to and from the plane.

Walk past two cottages on the left. To the left of a small, brick building, climb a stile and turn immediately left. Follow a track with a hedge on the right and a wire fence on the left. After about 100 yards, turn right opposite a wooden sign.

This is the point at which the canal terminated and the inclined plane began. The route of the incline has been landscaped to provide a pleasant yet historic woodland walkway.

8. Descend three wooden steps leading to a woodland path. You have now joined the site of the old inclined plane. At the bottom of the slope, emerge from the woodland and turn left, walking for about 200 yards up Cherry Tree Hill, and towards some brick cottages on the right-hand side of the road. Immediately after cottage number 7 turn right and descend a flight of brick steps. Walk along a path leading to a bridge over the railway line then a further bridge with iron railings which passes over a pool and waterfall.

New Pool was used in Abraham Darby's day as a back-up for the other pools in the dale which themselves helped power machinery in the iron-works.

9. For a brief diversion into a site of industrial history, continue ahead along the path from the pool for a few yards, then turn right at a T-junction. Almost immediately turn left up some steps at the side of a cottage. On

emerging on to a narrow, metalled lane, turn right by a collection of interesting buildings and gardens, including 'Woodside Cottages'.

The buildings include an old Victorian boys' school and a row of workers cottages still referred to as 'Engine Row'. Behind the school is the site of the Coalbrookdale Company's engine called 'Resolution' which once pumped water from the lower pools and up to the main Upper Furnace Pool at Coke Hearth.

Turn right and right again. This time, stay on the path ahead, which passes along the right-hand side of New Pool and then a stream. Keep straight ahead at all times. Later, the railway line can be seen on the left. At a wooden signpost, where the track becomes a well-made path, follow the 'Park Lane' sign. At a T-junction with Park Lane, turn left onto a metalled road.

The pathway which has brought you alongside the stream to this point has long been known as the 'Ginny Rails'. It is the track of the former, horse-drawn tramway which used to convey raw materials from the Lightmoor and Little Dawley areas to Coalbrookdale. It was once the driving force for waterwheels at both Lightmoor and Coalbrookdale.

10. Walk along the road and under the railway bridge towards the tall chimney stack at Lightmoor.

Lightmoor's fortune or misfortune as the case may be, was based on the fact that it sat on rich deposits of coal, iron-ore and clay which were rigorously exploited from the early eighteenth century until the mid-twentieth. Blast furnaces later arrived on the scene and a rash of workers' cottages. Shutfield was the big name for many years at Lightmoor. Shutfield Tileries operated here from about 1825 until 1950, making varied use of the local clays. One firm still makes bricks at Lightmoor today, but the rest of the area is still trying to recover from nearly three hundred years of pillage.

11. Near the top of the hill, look for and follow a tarmac pathway leading up to the main road on the right. Cross the main road and join another tarmac pathway opposite, climbing towards woodland. At a T-junction turn right along a

quiet, metalled lane through a short stretch of woodland. Pass 'Q.A. Kitchens' on the left and arrive at another Tjunction, and turn left.

'Q.A. Kitchens' stands at the Rudges on the site of the pool belonging to the Lightmoor Company (later taken over by the Coalbrookdale Company) which was used to power the Lightmoor Furnaces. Also nearby stood a small Wesleyan Chapel, colloqui-ally known as 'Fat Bacon' chapel because a pig was donated annually to celebrate the chapel's anniv-ersary.

Walk along the road for about 50 yards, passing the remains of some old brick stables on the right.

The row of stables was once the home of horses used to pull the tubs along the Coalbrookdale Company's tramways, down the Ginny Rails to Coalbrookdale, and also between the Shutfield Tileworks and the Lightmoor Tileworks.

12. Soon after passing the stables, turn right onto a pathway indicated by a wooden signpost pointing to 'Aquaduct' (sic). Follow the well-defined pathway which veers left, then takes you past a pool on the right before climbing between trees. Keep to the main pathway at all times, following the signposts to Aqueduct.

13. At a T-junction turn left, joining a pathway with a stream on the right-hand side. The path emerges into an open area, with the Wide Waters on the left. Walk straight ahead to the Car Park at Castle Pools.

It is worth exploring the nearby group of pools. They are relics of the industrial era and surrounded by grey, pit-banks. Landscaped some years ago with pathways and footbridges they form a pleasant semi-rural area. 'Castle Pools', are named after Dawley Castle, destroyed during the Civil War, but which once stood on a nearby hill opposite the parish church.

EXPLORING SHROPSHIRE
with Shropshire Books

BOOKS

UNDISCOVERED SHROPSHIRE
14 Walks in North Shropshire
Eve Powell

SHROPSHIRE WALKS WITH
WRITERS
Gordon Dickins and
Gladys Mary Coles

GREEN WALKS FROM
OSWESTRY
Mary Hignett

WALKS AROUND TELFORD
David Gregory

SHROPSHIRE WALKS BY THE
WATERSIDE
David Gregory

TEN WALKS THAT CHANGED
THE WORLD
Walks into Shropshire's Industrial Past
Kate and Keith Pybus

TOWN TRAILS

Bridgnorth
Ludlow
Much Wenlock
Oswestry

LEAFLETS

Bridgnorth
Market Drayton
Much Wenlock
Oswestry
Pontesbury
Stokesay
The Jack Mytton Way

CYCLE TRAILS

Cycling for Pleasure in the Marches

The Jack Mytton Way (Long distance
path for horses, cyclists and walkers)

For further details of these and many more books on Shropshire contact:

SHROPSHIRE BOOKS
The Annexe, Shirehall
Abbey Foregate
SHREWSBURY SY2 6ND
www.shropshirebooks.co.uk